Nine cups of Coffee & Two Scones

Conversations in a Teashop in The Upper Esk Valley on the North York Moors

Written by Georgina Truscott
from
audio recordings
made during 2001 - 2007

Published by Westerdale Publishers
In 2008

May 2008

Each Tuesday morning in the North Yorkshire moorland village of Castleton a group (about nine of them at a time) of older people meet in the Tea Shop to reminisce. People have also been recounting memories over cups of tea while sitting at home by the fire. A voice recorder has captured the conversations, painting a vivid picture of a way of life that has vanished. Here are their stories in the way they were told, either talking in their cottages or at the Tea Shop, Tuesday after Tuesday, meeting together and enjoying their order for "nine cups of coffee and two scones".

This is a happy book. These are stories recounted with happiness. Childhood and youth in the Upper Esk Valley during the twentieth Century are brought alive again. Memories differ and may not always be accurate, and where dates and names are left out it is usually because they have been forgotten. But as Emma Beeforth said, "In my life time I think there must have been more change than there'll ever be again, when life back then, as it was in the closed world of Westerdale, is compared with life now."

And Daisy Cornforth said, "Gosh, when you come to think, things have altered that fast!"

Stories Told

Conversations in Cottages

*An old postcard of Castleton. The building on the corner on the left is now **Castleton Tea Shop**.*
T Watson photographer WLPS

8

In 2005 the Civil Parish of Danby, in the Upper Esk Valley, *which includes Westerdale, Commondale, Castleton, Danby, Botton and Ainthorpe had a population of a little over two thousand people. The area from the source of the Esk to Glaisdale covers about sixty square miles. The stories begin in Westerdale, a small village community with a present population of around a hundred and fifty, at the head of the River Esk, twenty miles or so from where the river reaches the sea at Whitby. Westerdale is a string of cottages and scattered farms in a horseshoe shaped dale about six hundred feet above sea level, surrounded by moorland. Every way out of it is eventually uphill.*

School Days in Westerdale

In memories of around seventy years ago the grassy hill outside the little school at Westerdale was kept cut and green and beautiful. It was divided into the boys' and the girls' playground. The door into the schoolroom was where it still is (the school is now the Village Hall), and at that time there were two stoves in the long open schoolroom, one at the end and one in the middle. The middle one was an open fire with a great fireguard around it. If the children got wet coming to school in the morning the teacher would try to dry their coats by the fire. The numbers of children would vary between thirty to forty, from five years old to school leaving age, usually at fourteen, and there were two teachers. The teachers did look after them well, Bessie said, even though they

Westerdale schoolchildren in 1931
with teachers Miss Watson and Miss Mortimer
Back Row: *Cyril Ellerby, Les Bonas, Bill Hartley, Jack Hartley, Ben Smith, John Dowey, Joe Booth, Tom Mortimer, Fred Middleton*
Middle row: *Doris Lynas, Dorothy Taylor, Eileen Dowey, Eleanor Ellerby, Muriel Mortimer, Elsie Dowey, Peggy Ellerby, Emma Knaggs, Greta Dale, Mary Dale, Meg Booth, Bessie Flintoft.*
Front row: *Paul Hynson, Herbert Flintoft, Ian Hardisty, Tim Knaggs, George Booth, Bill Thompson, Stan Smith.*
(In 2007 eight of these children are still living in the Upper Esk Valley)

9

had a lot to do. The school toilets were in the yard beyond the school building, through a door where the kitchen sink is now. They were not flush toilets. They were buckets with toilet seats on. The two sets of school toilets were back to back, for boys and girls. Miss Dent was a teacher at Westerdale school in the 1920s. Elsie started school in 1924. If milk was brought in the teachers used to make Ovaltine and cocoa at morning playtime, though sometimes the bigger children made their own. Elsie said children brought milk straight from the cow. The children took their own food to school for their dinners.

The school day began at 9, and ended at 3.30 pm. In wintertime the children would leave a bit earlier to get home in daylight. There was no school transport. When there was a lot of snow on the ground Bessie's father used to come to meet her and her brothers with a horse and he put the three children on the horse to take them home.

On St George's Day, or "Royal Oak Day", all the children came to school wearing a piece of oak tree. But one year Bessie and her brother didn't wear any. Some of the boys beat them with nettles on their bare legs so badly that they had to be sent home. Bessie can still remember the pain! That was when Bessie was about nine or ten. The boys had been lying in wait with the nettles for anyone not wearing a piece of oak.

*Bessie
Flintoft -later
Underwood*

Bessie passed her eleven plus. She went to Lealholm to sit the second part of the exam. There was a grammar school at both Saltburn and Whitby, but Bessie's family lived at a farm right up at the top of the dale at Woodend in Westerdale. She could not go to grammar school because there was no transport even to get to Castleton station from Woodend. She said, "You had to pay for transport, uniform and books yourself. My family couldn't afford it." So she left school. Families who could afford to often boarded their children in Saltburn, and Jean Rook who was "evacuated" to Westerdale (and later was a famous journalist in Fleet Street) was one who boarded there. Avril Randles who at that time lived at High House in Westerdale had a pony to ride to Castleton so she could catch a bus to Saltburn Grammar School. Maybe she left her pony at the station.

Commondale Wesleyan Choir 1914

Castleton is a larger village in the Upper Esk Valley and it is the next along the river from Westerdale, 2 miles north east. It is largely strung out along the ridge high above the River Esk, though Castleton Moor station is in the bottom of the valley where the railway line runs beside the river.

Commondale is about 3 miles along the rail track NW from Castleton - a tiny village by Sleddale Beck. During the second half of the nineteenth century and until the 1950s it was a big, busy industrial community where a brick works brought prosperity.

At one time there were schools at Castleton and at Commondale as well as Westerdale. Commondale had Mr Pratt's Brick Works, so there were a lot of people living there. In later years Elsie's and Bessie's children went to Castleton School because Westerdale School closed in 1952. Colin Flintoft, Audrey Lister and Audrey

Shaw passed exams to go to the grammar school and that would only have left three or four children at the school, so it closed. For a year or two Westerdale had fewer children, but then there was "a boom" again.

Teachers usually stayed working in a school for a long time, but when Grace Watson got married she couldn't carry on teaching because married woman teachers were not allowed to work in Church of England schools, which Westerdale was. She married Harry Hardisty of Westerdale and they went to live at Bainbridge. She was able to teach there.

Bessie told how once she had stayed for a year with an aunt and uncle at Boroughbridge and she went to school there. It was the only time she ever had a school report. It was a wonderful report - she came top! Bessie has lived in the Esk Valley all her life except for that one year. She's lived in Castleton since 1951, and Elsie has since 1948.

Dancing

The village schools didn't have joint sports activities but the schools joined in the folk dancing festival at Whitby. Elsie remembers once dancing at a concert in the Institute, which was a "tin" (corrugated iron) Village Hall in Westerdale where Kestrel House is now. Linda remembers going to some very good parties there as a child, perhaps at Christmas. Elsie remembers some good dances there too. They cost sixpence to go, and Sandy Muir played in the band. His brother Jim played the piano accordion and saxophone and their Dad played the drums. Jack Hartley, Arthur Burke and Allen Jackson played too.

Westerdale School Folk Dancers at Whitby in the 1930s. Mary Dale (later Mould) now in her eighties, is 1st left, back row.

The "tin" Village Hall in Westerdale, sadly dilapidated in later years.

People walked miles to go to dances, and Elsie said they sometimes came home at three o'clock in the morning. They would walk home from Castleton or Danby or even Lealholm, wherever a dance had been held, and there might be a dozen or so people all walking home to Westerdale. There was once an article in the newspaper about noisy people walking home from dances back up the lane. Bessie said they'd get, "sort of paired off, and someone in front would shout, 'Are you coming?' They'd stopped for a ... whatever!!"

11

Dances in winter were always timed for a moonlit night - it would be frosty and bright. Bessie walked to dances in her boots, with her shoes in a bag, and has even been to a dance on her bike with her long dress tied around her waist! There was usually a supper. There was not much alcohol. Girls were not allowed to drink it - and they couldn't go into pubs in those days. There was sometimes a whist drive before the dance, and they often didn't finish until two o'clock in the morning. There was nice old-fashioned dance music to dance to, waltzes, foxtrots and so on.

Some memories of the Second World War

Derrick Champion told how during the war two bombs were dropped on Danby. They dealt with one, but the other mine kept sinking. The more they dug the more it sank until it was totally out of reach. It is still there today and a house has been built on it! He wouldn't say where. Elsie knows where it is too, but she's not saying either.

Bessie lived seven miles further down the River Esk from Castleton at Greenhouses near Lealhom, for a while. When the first German plane was brought down (by Captain Peter Townsend) near Sleights, outside Whitby, she saw it come down. She ran five miles to see it and to take a piece of the plane home for a souvenir. But when she got there they wouldn't let her have it. It was a long way to run, and a long walk back.

One night the bombers flew over and Bessie remembers that incendiary bombs were dropped just across from Greenhouses, some of them on a farm. The farm buildings were set alight. Bessie said the neighbours went to help to put the fires out,. They found there was a fire burning in the attic too, so they had to go and put that out. They went up the stairs, "And on the landing were a lot of 'jerries' full of .. you know what. So they took it and put the fire out with it! And that's a true story because my Dad was one of the people who did it."

Kitchings Shop and, further up, Watson's Butchers in 1908

Life in the valley wasn't really affected by the war very much. Just every now and then. Most were working in agriculture, a reserved occupation. Bessie said there was an early warning station at Danby Beacon and reports came from there of things happening, but Elsie said they didn't see much. There was a searchlight in Westerdale on Broadgate lane and one at Shaw End at Lealholm. When planes were about they could be seen in the searchlights. Linda Grout said George Booth tells a story about airmen coming down in a plane near Westerdale and going to his farm. George's family has been in Westerdale for generations. One night bombs fell on the moor near Westerdale.

They would sometimes see bomber planes going out at night and then hear them come back in the early hours. Elsie said they could see barrage balloons going up over Teesside, so they knew something was about to happen. There were no bunkers to hide in. Linda remembers Percy and Margaret Wilson telling a story about how, on their way walking back to Castleton from a domino drive at Commondale, German planes were flying over and dropping their bombs as they went home. Percy and Margaret had to roll into a ditch and hide while the bombs were exploding.

Castleton Cheese Fair

People had ration books, but those who lived on a farm were their own butchers. "We had a lot of friends, then!" said Bessie. They did some bartering. They had butter, eggs, their own bacon, and would kill a sheep. If people kept bees they were allowed an allocation of sugar for their bees. Elsie's family came from Hollins Farm on Westerdale Side. They made cheese and sold it at the Friday Cheese Fair in Castleton, near where the bank is now, and butter too that they'd made for different customers. Ernie Brown from Westerdale regularly took Hannah Mary Carr who worked for him, sitting up high on the very hard pillion seat of his motor bike to Castleton Cheese Fair or the station, laiden with two big heavy baskets full of cheese or butter. Kitching's shop in Castleton was where Elsie bought rennet for her cheese. Puckrins shop was up where the hairdressers now is, and Kerridges was above that. Elsie remembers going to a wooden hut near the British Legion building to have her hair cut, and there was another hut there for the cobbler.

Amy & Beanie Kitching, of Kitching's Shop, Castleton

13

A Skin Specialist, & Doctors and Nurses in General

Linda told how her Grandma had a skin rash that wouldn't go away so her mother took Grandma to see the doctor. He treated her for a week, but the rash did not improve so her mother took Grandma back to see him again. He said it was no good, her Grandma had better see a skin specialist. So Linda's mother took Grandma off to Carter Bequest Hospital in Redcar to see the skin specialist, and the specialist was their own doctor! He was now the specialist! Bessie remembers that happening to others. Linda remembered one doctor always gave people yellow pills or white pills. Bessie thought they were Smarties! This was in the early 50s. In earlier days there was Doctor Jack, who lived at Castle House in Castleton and rode a horse. Then there was another doctor who lived at Ainthorpe. When Emma was a child she hurt her leg while sledging. She got a big abscess above her knee, and that doctor came to Dibble Bridge and lanced it.

Bessie's brother Wilfred broke his elbow when they were children. It came better, but then it got worse. One day they were playing, taking turns to jump off a box. He was slow, so Bessie pushed him, and he fell and broke the elbow again. Someone had to walk all the way to Ainthorpe from Westerdale (4 miles) to fetch the doctor. There was no telephone, or car. Wilfred had to wait a long time until the doctor came, and he set it on the kitchen table. " If you saw Wilfred's elbow now you would realise why it is like it is. He can't bend his arm." For weeks Wilfred, who was only 6 or 7 when this happened, would say "I won't cry if you put the gramophone on." So Bessie had to sit with him and play the gramophone - to wind it up with the handle and change the needle. They had Sandy Powell's record "Can you Hear me Mother?" It was always on for Wilfred.

Bessie doesn't remember many people visiting the doctor because generally if people needed a doctor they asked him to come. Emma Skidmore remembers having to go to him, though. She was trying to do somersaults at school. She says she was never very good at it and got a "helping hand" from somebody who pushed her. Her thumb came out of joint so she was taken to the doctor to have it put back. He was a good doctor and he was kind. When people hadn't got much money he sometimes helped them along. People didn't go to the doctor often. Medical care was quite expensive, though farmers could perhaps pay "in kind", with a chicken or something like that if they couldn't afford the money.

Frances and Emma, the Featherstone sisters from the post office at Rose Cottage in Westerdale, were midwives and used to deliver babies. "They weren't qualified. They weren't even married!" said Bessie. "They delivered the letters too! Their mother used to go as well sometimes, but she wasn't qualified either. People used to book their mother for about a month after a birth to look after the family."

The Featherstone sisters delivered Emma Skidmore, her brother Joe and sister Mary, but by the time her brother Michael was born Nurse Phillips was working, and Michael was her first delivery in this area. Linda remembers that her grandmother got into trouble with Nurse Phillips for delivering a baby for Jennifer Champion, as though she could have stopped it!

Emma Featherstone and her brother Joe

Donkeys, and the Westerdale Blacksmith

In Westerdale Bessie's family looked after the Whitby beach donkeys for the winter times, as did other families. They could be yoked up to pull a little cart, or the children could ride them. Or they tipped them off!

There was an old wheel at Bessie's farm with a wheelhouse that had been used for grinding corn, with places where the horses were yoked up to pull it round. "When the donkey was sick of us it would shoot into the wheelhouse and go through the yokes and we would be knocked off. One of them was a terror for doing that! But the donkeys really were good. " They didn't need a lot of food. Some people had them to work, but Bessie's family didn't - they had them for pleasure. They had to be groomed, and looked after, but the family had free donkey rides. In Whitby they had to pay! There were lots of donkeys then on the sands, and their owners were grateful to have winter boarding for them. The Thompson family, the Doweys and other families had them too.

Bill Cockerill & his donkey

Harry Hardisty, John Hardisty's Grandad, was the Westerdale blacksmith then. He had a shop at the bottom of the High Street, with a joiner's shop next door. There were a lot of farriers then. The mill by the stream in Westerdale was working then, and people came to get their corn ground. The joiner's shop and the blacksmith's shop were a meeting place. There were usually two or three farmers there at a time gossiping and catching up with the news. When the Champions in Castleton had their garage down at the mill it was the same - a meeting place. There was a big stove to gather around.

Churches, Mr Punch, and Bad Lad Jack

The "Tin Church" was on Old Man's Park, and it was taken down after the new church was built. Some of the corrugated iron from which it was made was taken to make a garage up near Castleton School.

The Punch family from "Ellerstang" in Castleton bought the land where the "Tin Church" had been, and the Macmillan family put a wall

The old "Tin Church" undergoing demolition.
The site became Old Man's Park.

15

around the piece of land. A shop had been planned on the site, but the Punch family wanted the village to have it so they gave it to the village. Lord Downe gave other land for the new Castleton church and for the chapel and the village hall.

Mr Punch at "Ellerstang" had trees planted around his house so that he couldn't see any other buildings. He had a chauffer called Mercer. He used to say "Hoot, Mercer, hoot!" Mercer lived at Castle House. The Mercers had buildings along the road uphill from the church, where Emma Skidmore's garage is now, and there were Doug Jeffrey's sheds, and more along that side, and the fields behind. There was a cow byre, and milk used to go on the stand. Doctor Jack had the buildings and land before the Mercers. "Piper's Row" was opposite

Castleton Church when new, with "Piper's Row" in the foreground

the church (Mary Hartley later lived in the cottage on the end) and tiny Rose Cottage, once a home, was in the field beyond. It now has animals in it and it's a long time since it was a house. Dr Jack kept his horses in the field .

Remembering earlier years of the family who had the butcher's shop in Castleton until recently, Derrick said that going back 60 years or so, Charlie Watson was a big man. He got so wide that when he died in a room upstairs above the butcher's shop they couldn't get him downstairs. They had to put two big old army wagons that Derrick had bought under the window. They got Charlie out of the window onto one, and then down onto another to get him away. The Watsons used to deal in pigs and had a piggery down near Kitchings, up from the Mill. The pigs had to be kept in the field for a month, because of the twenty-eight day licence. There were licences even then. Tom, the butcher's lad, looked after the pigs until they were ready to kill. He kept them in a pigsty and he would feed them up until they were wanted. He fed them through a hole from outside the sty. "Tom once put food in and then next day he put more in, and again more in each day, until he found round the other side the food was running out of the door. He looked in and the pig wasn't there. He hadn't realised the pig had been taken out and killed!" Tom's family had land behind Ellerstang. They used to put the waste there from the butcher's shop. Derrick remembers once Tom was coming up the road from there and he tapped on Billy Taylor's door and his foot went through it! Billy Taylor knew who'd done it and went up to the butcher's shop. A bit was stopped out of Tom's wage packet for a while.

Derrick told a story about "Bad Lad Jack". "At one time they made bricks at Ainthorpe as well as at Commondale. Bad Lad Jack lost his finger at Ainthorpe brick works. That was young Bad Lad. I told you how he got his name didn't I? Well when his father was a lad they lived at Commondale and he was working there on the pug machine, which mixes up the wet clay to make it smooth. Well a pig had pigged up at farm and there was a few little dead pigs you see, so he chucked them in amongst the clay. They turned out on the fence where they made bricks. It got back to the boss about this so his Mother had to go to a meeting (I don't know if he had a Dad or not). She kept saying, "You are a bad lad, Jack!" and it stuck with him forever after that and it rubbed of onto young Bad Lad his son, and so they were all called Bad Lad!"

Mrs Alexander's Well, and the "Listening Post"

Archie Alexander used to come around for orders for the shop. His wife was a Gibson. George Gibson was the landlord of Downe Arms in 1969 when Archie's wife Mrs Alexander was 100. She nursed Linda's baby daughter Maria, and played the piano at her hundredth birthday party. There was a well found behind Mrs Alexander's house, opposite Champion's garage. The soil was a different colour so they dug down and down and found the well. There were half a dozen gateposts covering it. There were chisel marks around the stone sides of the well. Mrs Alexander didn't remember it being there, so it must have been old. The vicar, David Adams, went down a ladder and found just a few broken pots down there - it was dry. Twenty yards up the road at the school there were water troughs full of water!

Castleton is a long row of buildings strung along a high ridge, and there is sand at the school side of Castleton, down even as far as Ellerstang. From the top of Castleton under the Moorlands Park side there is hard stone. Linda pointed out that the names of the houses on the sandy, wet side of the road, for example "Springfield" must be so for that reason. Derrick said that when somebody wanted to build a house behind the police house they couldn't put the foundations in because the ground is sandy and unstable. Eventually a bungalow was built on a raft. When they extended the bungalow towards the school they came on a spring of water running "thick as your wrist", and they had to drain it down into the field.

The "Listening Post" at the top of Westerdale Side was remembered. The "Observer Corps", which was different to, but similar to the Home Guard, used it in the Second World War. Marjory Mould and Dorothy Booth were cadets in the Observers. On nights off or after training the Observers came into the Downe Arms. Percy Wilson was one, and also Dick Harland, who now lives in Whitby. Harry Williamson was a chief officer.

Both Bessie and Emmas' fathers were in the Home Guard. They don't know what their fathers would have done if anything had happened! Bessie said her Dad didn't know his left from his right, for doing drill. There was someone in the Home Guard who farmed at Commondale. "The Home Guard met one night at Castleton and this farmer from Commondale got lost walking the few miles home afterwards. He ended up at Lockwood Beck. He'd never been as far as White Cross in his life! He'd never been anywhere. "

Westerdale Home Guard, with the "tin" Village Hall beyond

Games, and some Duties of a Taxi Service

Westerdale School

Games in the school yard at Westerdale were talked about - marbles and skipping, cricket and rounders, and "Fox Off". This was a game like Hide and Seek. One person would run off and the others would give them so long, then go and find them. Elsie said that the children weren't "tied in" to the school grounds at dinnertime, so they could go off and play. For an hour they had the freedom of Westerdale. They used to make slides down the steep hill behind the school, and they often played rounders on the School Hill. Donald Ellerby could hit the ball right over the Institute (the "tin Village Hall"), or, Emma said, into the churchyard the other way, so that they would have a job finding it. People tried hard to get Donald Ellerby on their side. Bessie said that one day a cricket ball was hit through a window from the front of the school room and out through a window at the back into the churchyard, "so that was two panes of glass gone". Cricket was off for quite a long time. They had to save up their pennies until the damage was paid for. It took a long time!

They took their own dinners and Bessie said milk, if it wasn't sour, or maybe cocoa. Emma said she and her friends sat on the quoit box to eat their dinners. Bessie said they sometimes might forget to go back into school! The bell would go, so they knew they should but perhaps didn't.

When Bessie was at school at Lealholm the children used to go to the cricket field to play cricket in their lunch time. Their teacher used to go to the Board Hotel for his lunch, so it might be after half past one before they were back in school!

Linda told how Annie Watson has said that in winter when she was a kid she used to set off on a sledge at the top of the long street down Castleton, and then if you were lucky you got almost to Danby before you stopped! In Westerdale, Emma said, they could sledge from high up Sugar Loaf Hill, right down all the way through to the bottom of Westerdale village.

Miss Watson with Westerdale School in about 1935. Bessie is 2nd from left near Miss Watson, middle row

Derrick Champion said the best sledging in Castleton was down Duckets Lane - you could get to the bottom of Ellerstang. One boy did that on a Norwegian sledge that he'd borrowed from the people who lived at Dibble, and he cut his knee badly. He lived at Huckaback, and his parents didn't know where he was. Derrick's father, who ran a taxi service from the garage in Castleton, had to go and break the news to his parents and take the boy to hospital.

Derrick said that as a taxi service they often had to do the hospital jobs, taking people there. It was often the only transport there was. They also had sometimes to bring a person back in a coffin. They had a car with seats that could be removed so that they could fit a coffin in. They even went to Leeds, and all over the area. Emma said they took her to hospital when she had her daughter, and Bessie said Arthur Champion took her to Whitby when she had her baby. Derrick Champion, in his eighties, took Emma Scarth from Bagdale to her wedding in Westerdale in July 2007.

Cricket, Pubs and a Hunt Ball at Rosedale

Derrick talked about cricket, and said that Castleton Cricket Team always wanted to win. "Old Fred Flintoft used to send his car to Darlington and all around to pick posh players up to come to play for Castleton. Joe Barker was one. He used to live down by the station but then he went to Darlington to work so Fred would send a car for him and for others. It was serious stuff. There weren't so many local players any more. George Flintoft was umpire and, at the "Henry Flintoft Cup", for every one he gave out he got a pint of beer that night!"

Fred was from a different Flintoft family to Bessie. Derrick said old Fred only had one eye. When he drove the car he used to take young Monty Pearson with him, to tell him whether there was a car coming. They were going along the road to Danby one day and Monty said, "There's a car coming Mr Flintoft." Fred said, "All right, lad." They kept going and going, and got nearly to Danby. Then Fred said "Where's that ... car gone?" Monty said, "It's gone past!"

Bessie said she remembers when Fred was out shooting at Broadgate. "Yes", said Derrick, "He nearly took all his buttons off his waistcoat that day!" Fred's gun went off as he was getting over a stile. They brought him in to Broadgate and the doctor had to be fetched.

Fred had hurt himself but he was lucky it wasn't worse. He was manager at the Quarry for a sand company.

Castleton Cricket Team in 1920

One day they wanted a little bag of sand to be sent for a special job down at Redhill in the south of England, and they sent Derrick all the way to Redhill on a Bank Holiday with the bag of sand. Fred built the house "Stoneleigh". Miss Flintoft had the farmhouse at "Park Nook". Then Fred married Miss Punch.

"Old Man's Park", Castleton. Mr George Flintoft, Mr Verril, Mr King, Mr Jack Farrow, Willie Hicks, two Atkinson brothers (the second named Will) and Mr Dowey

On Old Man's Park every day there were at least half a dozen men. They would go for a walk and then go back to the seat on Old Man's Park and reminisce. It was a meeting place. All the farmers used to stop there too when they came to the bank. Mr Mason, Mr Codling, Mr Atkinson, Harry Cook, Albert Gray, Walter Fishpool, David Hartley, and Arthur Cook. Often the men would call at the Downe Arms. They played dominoes nearly every lunchtime.

Snow clearing by White Cross in 1947, when coats were draped on the tops of protruding telegraph poles while the men shovelled.

Arthur Cook came from West House at the bottom of the hill on the way from Westerdale to the Commondale to Kildale road. Bessy says she still plays dominoes on a Friday night with Arthur 's same domino set, in its tin box. He had them when he came in the late sixties to live by the garage at Castleton. Derrick said that when Mrs Cook died at West House there was a snowstorm. There were roadmen on Sleddale Bank between Commondale and

Kildale trying to keep the road clear. He said, "We got the taxies to the farmhouse, but the hearse hadn't arrived. It was really difficult to get through the snow. We waited and waited. Old Arthur said, 'Well. Can't you put her in the back of the car?' The hearse came in the end."

Derrick said that Arthur would order a taxi to take him home from Castleton at half past eleven at night, but the drivers used to wait for hours and hours for him to come out of the pub. He used to play dominoes over lunchtime. Derrick said there was often more beer drunk over a lunchtime than in half a week - lots of them used to meet - Fred Flintoft, Frank Flintoft, Jim McNeil, Albert Gray, Dave Hartley, Walter Fishpool. In earlier years there was Willie Watson, then there was Teddy and Tim. Emma said Teddy Watson used to come every day. Derrick said that Teddy was a great character. Derrick said he was as blind as a bat!

Some men went to the pub on horseback. Bessie said that Frank Flintoft's Dad lived at Fryup and he was one who came to the Fox and Hounds at Ainthorpe on his horse. There was a stable at the back of the Downe Arms in Castleton. When it was time to go, the horses knew the way and would take their riders home. Derrick said once, down at the Eskdale pub near the station, some lads put the shafts of a cart through a gate, and then attached the horse on the other side! Linda said she thought people made their own fun and entertainment much more in those days. Lots of pranks went on. Elsie said it was really all harmless fun. Horses had a hard

A horse & cart in earlier years

job pulling carts on the hills around the area. Derrick said they often saw them "down" in the road because they hadn't been loaded properly. Horses had a job to do, though, and it wasn't for fun, as it is nowadays. Derrick had a donkey and cart. His Grandad shod the donkey with proper studs in its shoes. Derrick had no more bother with that donkey.

Derrick told a story of a Hunt Ball in Rosedale, back in the thirties. The "Purple Service Bus" bringing people back afterwards got stuck in the snow by the Fryup guide post, "Fat Betty", between Rosedale and Ralphs Cross high on the moor.

The next day Fred Hodgson and Bill Tyreman walked up there because they thought they'd get the bus out, but they couldn't. They found that old Dr Jack on his horse had been the first to get there. They had to use horses and sleds to get the occupants out. The bus was there for three days.

1933 - The stranded bus from the Rosedale Hunt Ball

The lost bus in January 1933 - the story told by Mary Mortimer of Westerdale

It was the night of the Hunt Ball in Rosedale. The snow, dry and powdery, lay very deep but it wasn't actually snowing when my brother, Frank Mould, and my sister Annie with her boy friend John Helm, set out from our home at Plumtree Farm in Danby Dale in Walter Green's bus from Danby to go to Rosedale Abbey for this great event which started with a meal and finished with dancing till midnight. Because of the weather my father had tried to stop them from going but they got their own way and sensibly set out well shod (Annie even had on a pair of Prussian boots) with coats, caps, gloves and scarves. Their dancing shoes were in their pockets. The bus was full of young people from Lealholm, Danby, Castleton and Commondale all clad in their best frocks and shoes.

They arrived at Rosedale Abbey in time for the dinner at 7.00 but noticed that it had started snowing again and was blowing hard. At midnight when they got into the bus to come home the wind was fierce and it was still snowing. The bus got up Knott Bank with some difficulty but got stuck soon after. There they all were at 1.00 in the morning with no food, nothing to drink and, worst of all some had no warm clothes.

My brother Frank thought he could lead the way across the moor to the head of Danby Dale using his shepherding knowledge of the moor and his long, stout stick. Annie and John followed. The others just stayed on the bus thinking that someone would soon come and rescue them.

By 8.00 am the three walkers had reached Stormy Hall and the gale had abated. Frank stopped off there (his place of work), had a cup of tea and immediately got on with his jobs! Annie and John walked on to Plumtree where John left to go across the dale to his work. Mary's father walked to all the farms on the West side of Danby Dale to raise the alarm. Meanwhile Annie changed into dry clothes, had some breakfast, set off down Church Bank and then along to the Davison Homes (in Ainthorpe) where she was

working. On the way she knocked and banged on every door she came to. Dr Jack (Alexander) rose to the occasion magnificently and rode the length of Castleton knocking and banging on every door telling people to bring horses, sledges, hot drinks, food and blankets up the Rigg and across along the Rosedale road. My brother Robert and I walked up our intake fields to watch the rescue expedition, led by Dr Jack on his old black nag, travelling along Castleton Rigg.

When they started to come back with the bus passengers on sledges and horseback it was already getting dark. The last people rescued didn't reach their homes until 7.00pm. There had been no way of keeping warm. They even burnt their dance programmes and music! They had been so cold that Dr Jack said they were in grave danger of hypothermia or even frostbite. Two lasses from Commondale took months to recover from their ordeal.

Dr Jack Alexander

Family life, and the Post and Telegram Services

Derrick's Grandad was one of a family of twenty-four children. Only one child died young - all the others lived well into their eighties! Grandad, a blacksmith all his life, was ninety-seven when he died. The family lived in a two up, two down cottage called the "Croft" in Rosedale. The children used to sleep top to toe, "Like little pigs, noddy arsey," Derrick said. The children went to work when they were twelve or thirteen.

Mother had a lot of cooking to do, though the older girls helped. The family often ate rabbit pie. They had a baking day each week, and they made cheeses and preserves. Housewives would buy a ten stone sack of flour and have a big bin to put it in. They would make bread, and teacakes, and put the loaves in tins in front of the fire to rise. Bread making was a daily chore. Bessie said Monday was washing, Tuesday was churning day to make the butter, Wednesday was bedroom day. Thursday was baking day. Friday was clearing up day and a Saturday was black leading day. On Sunday you only did the essential chores, and went to Chapel or Church two or three times. They went to the Service, home again, and then back to Sunday School. The children were given a little book with stamps in every week for good attendance at Sunday School. They were very pretty stamps. Bessie, Elsie and Emma still have their Good Attendance stamps, and Bessie still has her father's bible from when he was a child, and her husband Reggie's and an Uncle's.

Mr & Mrs Albert Gray
(nee Codling)

In those days the postmen used to walk on their rounds, and Elsie said your postman would do bits of shopping for you, and bring it the next day. Albert Gray from Castleton used to be the postman for Westerdale. Jimmy Hill did Rosedale. Derrick said Jimmy Hill would set off from the Abbey in Rosedale and begin by walking three miles to Thorgill, and then he'd walk around the whole dale and even up to the Lion pub on Blakey Rigg. He had to go within a whistling distance of every house every day, even if he had nothing for them, so that if people had letters or packages to post he could take them. Bessie said that in Westerdale Albert Gray went up as far as Esklets and Pyethorn. The Postmen walked their rounds, until Albert Gray got the first Post Office bike, which was there when Bessie's husband Reg started work as a postman in 1960.

Reg did his rounds in his own vehicle because he'd had an accident. Bessie said that then when the post arrived on the train in those earlier days there was maybe half a sack of it - not like now. There was no junk mail. When Reg first started there were only two telephone directories to take to Westerdale. One was for George Mortimer and one was for the Post Office. Nobody else had a phone. When he finished in 1983 there were only two people in Westerdale who hadn't got a phone. George Booth was one, and Lizzie Featherstone at "Firtrees" had no phone, electricity, toilet or water when she died at ninety-two in 1989. The first telephone Exchange was at Castleton Post Office. There was a board put up, and phone lines could be plugged in. Further away, for example at Baysdale Abbey, people used telegrams. Derrick, in his work as a taxi service, delivered many telegrams to Baysdale Abbey.

At the top of Castleton, Derrick left, with a horse drawn sledge, to pull milk cans or stone

Derrick said that in lots of cases telegrams brought bad news. If someone had died the envelope had a black border around it. He would have to hand it in and wait to see if there was any return telegram that was to be sent. It would be called a "bidding" message, for people to know they should come to the funeral.

Bessie said that they didn't have telephones when Reg, her fiancé at the time, came home on leave from the army in the winter of 1946-7. He sent a telegram from Liverpool to say he'd docked and would they have a taxi waiting for him at Castleton station. But the Esk Valley was knee deep in snow. Alan Medd had to walk with the telegram from Castleton. There were hardly any trains running from Grosmont up to Castleton. When Reg got to Grosmont there wasn't a train running. So they went to meet him with a horse and sledge. "He couldn't believe it - he'd come from Palestine!" Some of Bessie's family worked for the Council and were digging snow that year. Reg did too while he was on leave from the army and bought Bessie her engagement ring for fifteen pounds with the money he earned. It was a lot of money then, to spend on an engagement ring.

A Butcher's Revenge

Frank Farrow was a butcher. He began with a story about a butcher at Ugthorpe who was reported to the Ministry of Food for a prank he played on a customer who he got tired of. The customer came into the shop every day for a pork pie, but for some reason this man had irritated the butcher. So the butcher made a special pork pie, which looked just right, but inside he'd lined it with pig's hair and put in all the worst little bits and covered them with jelly to disguise it and baked it. It looked good, but it wasn't! He was "A beggar for tormenting people!" The awkward customer never went back for another pork pie.

Frank said there were some "Queer tricks, pig killing!" Johnny Cockerill was killing a pig down at the Mill. The pig was squealing before they gave it a bang on the nose to 'put it out' before they killed it. Tommy heard the pig squealing, and said, "Hey Johnny, could you come and kill a pig for me?" There was a pig that he wanted killing 'on the quiet'. Johnny couldn't say no to anybody, so, after he got the butcher's job done with Frank, they

Castleton butcher Charlie Watson, right, with Tom Armstrong and Ernie Watson.
Notice the meat in the open shop window.

went with Tommy to see to the pig. It was a great big black and white boar. "As soon as they got there Tommy cleared off into the house! Johnny only had a 2-2 rifle instead of the proper gun to use, and he said to Frank, "When you hear the rifle cock, open the door." Frank heard the rifle cock. He opened the door, and out shot the pig across the farmyard and into a hayshed and disappeared. Tommy came out and said, "What's on?" The cat was out of the bag then, because they had to clear out all the straw to get the pig out!"   In those days slaughtering was all done on the butcher's premises. All animals including cattle were stunned and shot, what Frank called "pole-axed". There were no refrigerators. Meat kept better in hot dry weather than it did in muggy weather. Sunshine in hot weather sealed the meat and turned it black, and with that seal on it the flies couldn't damage it. Kidneys and other meat had plenty of fat left on them in those days, which kept the flies off too. They used to put pepper on it. Derrick said there was a man called Charlie who had a cat o' nine tails, and he killed bluebottles with that!

Bessie said that bacon was cured at home. There were sides of bacon hung up in the kitchen on hooks, and there was mesh on the kitchen windows to keep out flies. Derrick said you had to dodge the sides of bacon when you were in the kitchen. Frank said meat was good in those days.

Derrick said that in the old days they used to buy a couple of old sows that were "as thin as rattle snakes" after they'd had a litter. They were fed with as much as they would eat, and their weights would get up to as much as forty stone! It was all good fresh meat, but nowadays that pork would be condemned - you are not allowed to produce such meat because it was fat. Derrick bought an acre of potatoes from Johnny Cockerill. Johnny harvested them and then Derrick led them home in a cart to feed to his pigs. He cooked the potatoes in a huge copper that took about five hundredweight at a time. Derrick took the pigs to Jack Watson's shop at Danby to be killed, and Jack wouldn't believe Derrick had fed them on nothing but potatoes. Frank said that Bill Thompson kept pigs, and the last pig he killed was a big one. He "finished them up" on potatoes and a bit of barley meal. "This last one was thirty stones of pig and had a very wide back. When it was split open there was an inch of lean to ten inches of fat! Brenda didn't have to buy any fat for two or three years. She did all her baking with it, and Bill had scrapings for his meals; breakfast, dinner and tea and supper, for weeks, just eating fat. It did them no harm! People ate a lot of rabbits too, though."

At Charlie's at Danby Lodge they killed six pigs a year. Frank said when you came in for your meal at 7 o'clock, because that was mealtime at Danby Lodge then, there was a table that was scrubbed white. There was no tablecloth. There was a big plate of dry bread on the table. "Then Aunt Ada would come in with a great pot dish, full just with fried

Danby Lodge

25

bacon, cut up to half an inch thick. We would all be at the table, (there were four children at home at Danby Lodge then), and you took your fork and leaned across the table and stuck it in your bacon and took it out, and it dripped with fat. You ate it just with dry bread, no butter because you didn't need it. What harm did it do? You were hungry, and you ate it. There was nothing else! It was good pure food." Lots of people ate bread and dripping.

There were not many pheasants on the moor. When Derrick took on Westerdale Shoot there were about thirty-odd birds taken a year. The farmers couldn't shoot on the moor. People on rented farms were not allowed to shoot pheasants because they belonged to the landlord. Frank thinks it's still the same with rabbiting today. People only ate chickens, "boilers", when they were old and past laying.

Castleton Show

Castleton Show, in 1924

At one time Castleton Agricultural Show was held behind Castleton Chapel, and there was a flower show behind Ellerstang, on Punches' land. There were hound trails. Castleton Show has been running for about 110 years. For the 'Show Centenary' people dressed up in old-fashioned costumes. Emma Skidmore found the date of the first show in an old book, so that's how they knew it was the Centenary. In the days when the show was held behind Castleton Chapel people used to walk all the animals to it, even from Glaisdale. There are no longer sheep at the Show, though there are still horses.

The Show was held in a field that was reached by a driveway between the buildings near the Downe Arms. Heavy horses could get through, but when large wagons began to be used they couldn't get them between the buildings so the Show was moved from

Emma Thompson (later Skidmore) with Jean Rook, collecting for the Red Cross.

Castleton to Danby. The Show has grown since it moved, although when it was at Castleton there used to be a little grandstand. The schools entered paintings and collages and handwriting. There was a fair with coconuts shies, and swings on Primrose Hill and in the main street at the same time.

For the Coronation the children marched down the village from the school with Mr Finlay in front. Linda Grout's house used to be a public hall in addition to the village hall - known as the "New Hall" and they met there. Linda's house is now called "Dawnay Hall" after a soldier who was killed in the First World War, and in whose memory the "New Hall" was built. Pam remembers the "New Hall" being used by the school, and Emma remembers the first Cricket Club dinners being held there, and the Farndale Hunt Balls. Those were big occasions, with long dresses, and people all dressed up. There was a Glaisdale Hunt Ball too.

Emma remembers once walking a mile back home from a Hunt Ball at New Hall to Dibble Bridge and feeling so tired she decided to lie down on her bed in her long frock for just a few minutes before getting ready properly for bed. She woke up the next morning, still in her long frock! "It was blue, with a frill on."

Children

People were used to walking. Children thought nothing of walking two or three miles to school every day, whatever the weather. Emma Thompson (now Skidmore) walked for years two miles from Dibble Bridge to Westerdale Church twice on Sundays, and to Westerdale School every day, because she didn't want to go to Castleton School. Emma's father worked at the farm at Dibble, and the family lived in the bungalow there.

Eva, Herbert, Mary & John Henry Featherstone lived at Cockle House Farm

When she was a young girl Elsie Mould used to play the organ in Westerdale Church, and Emma used to sit in the organ box with her. The Vicar was always late. Once the two girls were in the organ box and as usual Mr Dickie, the Vicar, was late. After a while everything had gone very quiet, so they peeped out of the box and found that everybody had given up waiting and had gone home and only they were left! So they left too. They met Mr Dickie coming along the path to the church, but they didn't stop. Everybody else had gone! "The Vicar only lived across the road and the bells would have rung for him to hear. He was a tall man, over six feet tall, with long legs and a big stride, but his long legs didn't get him there any quicker".

Emma and her Mum used to clean the church. Emma and her sister Mary had to go back on Saturday afternoons to dust it. They were frightened of the mice so they were "timid with the duster". The mice ate the keys on the organ. The church was warm because Emma's Dad used to light the big stove at the back on a Saturday night ready for Sunday. He rang the bells for about fifty years, and he dug the graves for thirty-five.

Alice & George Thompson lived at Riddings, Dale Side, Westerdale

The children used to go "Shouting". The girls did it on New Years Day and the boys on Christmas Morning. The girls used to chant,

"It was by chance, that I came here,
To wish you this morning, a Happy New Year.
I can't stay long, must quickly shift,
So please will you give me my New Year's gift!"

The boys shouted,

"I wish you a merry Christmas,
a Happy New Year,
Good luck with all you have, all through the year.
So please will you give me my Christmas Box!"

The tradition goes back generations. If you were the first child to reach a house you got a piece of silver. Emma said if you just got copper you knew someone had beaten you to it. There was often a piece of cake or ginger bread and a piece of cheese given to them.

Emma used to set off on New Years Day at six o'clock in the morning when it was still dark. "Going down Christygate with my torch shining, every little thing that moved made me jump." She started at Lister's on Westerdale Side. If Mr Lister wasn't yet up he'd throw Emma sixpence out from the bedroom window. Then Emma would go right up past Elsie's to the head of the dale, then down into Broadgate and to the village. By the time she got into the village she would only get a halfpenny. Emma's last call was usually at the Featherstones at Church Farm, to Uncle John, Liza, Emma, and George Willie. John Featherstone was Elsie's Dad's uncle, and Emma said, "He was everybody's' Uncle John, wasn't he!" The Featherstones had lots of dogs. She would knock at the door and then stand well back till the dogs were controlled. The children didn't keep the money for themselves. They took it back home and it might buy some shoes or other necessities. They would probably keep the cake or cheese for their family, depending on where they got it from - if it was very good they would eat it themselves!

The children used to stand on the church wall when the plums were ready and jump down quickly into the garden of Church Farm and run to grab a couple of plums.

Elsie Mould's Great Uncle John Featherstone & his dogs

They hoped the dogs wouldn't get them. It's a high wall! The keeper, Robert Kerr, lived at the bottom of the village. They had no children there, so he used to give pears and other fruit to the village children. Emma picked wild flowers to send to her Grandma in Newcastle. The children picked primroses, and there were always wild flowers for Mothering Sunday. At school there used to be occasions when the children would be given a prize for the one who picked the most flowers. They also pressed the flowers and stuck them into little scrapbooks. Emma won a brooch, and then Doris Milner who lived at Riddings won one the next time.

Memories of happy childhoods were clouded by difficulties of others - there was a story that in some families in the Upper Esk Valley poverty was so severe that a mother might come to a school gate to breastfeed her hungry infant school child.

Fuel

Elsie Mould's father, Albert Dowey, was born in 1890. He used to go "turf cutting" to the turf moor on Westerdale moor, and she has a very good photograph of him (shown). He took a spade over his shoulder, and the sack hanging from it contained his "bait", as his lunch was called. Derrick commented that Elsie's Dad would have known to come home from the turf moor for his dinner, when the buzzer blew at Rosedale Mines! At that time Elsie's family was living at Hollins Farm on Westerdale Side.

The farms in Westerdale have "turf rights", and the farmers cut the turfs from the moor every year for fuel. Turf and peat cutting rights for digging or cutting were granted by the landowner. Some people used to go up to a peat moor up in Fryup Dale. John Greg and John Thompson still go now, in 2006. Peat Cutting is digging peat out of a pit, rather than taking turfs off the surface. Emma Skidmore said there were turfs in the coalhouse when they moved into Castle Cottage in Castleton.

Albert Dowey, Elsie's father, going turf cutting

Sticks and turfs were the fuel used for fires and ranges. Bessie's father once bought a ton of coal for five shillings from somebody who came round and wanted to get rid of it. "My mother played war!" she said. "Fancy wasting money on that!" Though Bessie said the ton of coal lasted a long time.

Emma remembers going to Hall Woods in Westerdale for oven sticks. They were twigs and long pieces of fallen branch to put on the stick heap. Bessie said they used to have a sheep dog which loved to go with them to fill an old upright pram with sticks, and the dog would be harnessed to the pram to pull it home! Emma said she carried oven sticks from Dibble Bridge for years after they were married, for their side oven. Elsie said they also used to go to the moor for "gowlings", the long sticks of burnt off heather. They made very good kindling. They were also sent out as children to collect fuel. They'd wrap a band around the gowlings to bring them back. Derrick said he used to bundle them up himself, and they weren't very heavy to carry home.   Bessie said that was how they filled their time in, in those days, doing things to help their parents. Emma agreed, remembering carrying the milk up to Bagdale from Town Farm.

Bessie says she often went up to the moor with her father to "rickle" the turf, standing two turfs up together then putting another on top, so they would dry out. Then they would be put into a stack. They might dry in a week if the weather was good. Otherwise they took longer. They were cut in June or July, after hay time. There were proper spades to dig the turfs out. A peat spade was different, because it was narrower than the wide turf spade. When the turfs were dry they would be brought down from the moor on a sledge pulled by a horse.

Bessie Flintoft (later Underwood), her brother Herbert and parents Elsie & Wilfred in 1928 collecting peat from Westerdale Moor with horses and sledge

There was no electricity. They used candles and oil lamps. 'Tilley lamps' came in eventually. Emma says they didn't have a Tilley lamp until they went to live at Haggerback. They bought candles from the Co-op, or from Kerridges. Then there were "Aladdin", or mantle lamps. Bessie said they got a generator in 1946. It just powered electricity for their own farm. When the generator was switched off all the lights went out, so the last one to bed had to switch it off! Bessie said, "We thought we'd got everything then, even though it was just lights." Derrick at Esk Mill lived in the first house in Castleton to have electricity. It was taken from the water mill. They charged two pence for people to charge their batteries there. He said that batteries were in a glass dome.

It would have been well into the 1950s before electricity got as far as Broadgate Farm in Westerdale. Westerdale High Street was connected up in about 1954. Emma said that was the year she was married. Linda said she couldn't remember having electricity at Daleside. Linda Grout lived at Daleside Farm in Westerdale until 1963. She said it was a lovely place to live. Water was from a spring at the side of the hillside and her Dad tapped it into the kitchen where there was a bath with a flap that folded down to be a worktop during the week. They had a bath once a week "if they were lucky". When the spring dried up in the summer they went through a gate at the bottom of the field to another good spring, and they took milk churns to get the water. There was no electricity for most of the time they were there, and they used lamps. Linda said, "You walked down the side of the building and the loo was there. All the other buildings were for animals." They had a couple of cows and pigs. The toilets were buckets with toilet seats on. Every now and then the buckets were emptied onto the midden along with the animal dung.

Hay time

The Flintoft family harvesting at Leith House high in Westerdale in 1935.
Bessie is the little girl in a sunhat, with her father Wilfred, her mother Elsie, her
Aunt Aida, and her Grandmother.

Hay time was when the midges used to bite, and everyone had to help. Hay timing was a work of art, Bessie said. Turning the hay first, and then raking it into wind-rows, the long rows that Derrick said needed to be forked up so that the rain ran off, before the hay was made into haycocks. Linda can remember making haycocks in Westerdale. Some people had horse drawn hay rakes. These were also used to "clean rake", to gather up what was left behind. Derrick said that lots of farm fires in those days were caused by damp hay over heating, and firing.

Elsie and Bessie didn't like going up onto the top of the hay stacks, but Bessie remembered that in later years Hilda had a daughter who, when she was only four or five, was terrified of heights. She was pushed by her younger sister up a twenty-one rung ladder onto the top of a hay stack. Hilda looked up and saw two little faces looking down. She said, "What did you do?" and her younger daughter said, "I just pulled her up!" Hilda couldn't understand how she had got the bigger one up there, because she was really frightened. "But the younger daughter would be the boss. She was never frightened of anything."

Sheep

Hilda's farm at Broadgate in Westerdale still has sheep rights on the moor, though they haven't many sheep out nowadays. Everyone agreed that it's a shame there are fewer sheep on the moor now. Hilda said that there are a lot of trees growing there that in the past would have been eaten down by the sheep. Elsie said that "we don't see the quality of sheep round here on the moor any more either."

Tups at Broadgate, Westerdale, with Grandad Flintoft

Derrick said there isn't such a thing as "a shepherd" around here now. He said that years ago you had to seek permission to put sheep on the cricket field, for so many weeks a year. At the end of that time you would not see the sheep coming back over the bridge to the cricket field again because they were shepherded every day and kept away. Bessie said there were never sheep grazing in the village in past times like there are now. The shepherds kept them out. People were *farming*, and they took time to do it. It was part of their daily tasks.

Hilda remembered that Grandad Flintoft had sheep, and her husband Herbert had to learn to look after them when he was young. They used to dip them, and when Herbert was older they would walk miles around the moor every day to check them. In later years Hilda went with Herbert in the Landrover up to the moor once to look for some sheep. They went up towards Ralphs Cross. He parked the Landrover and said, "Wait there." So Hilda waited. He didn't come back, and he still didn't come back, so Hilda stood on the top of the Landover to see if she could see him. She looked all around but she couldn't see him. She stayed up there waiting for another hour, and then thought, "Blow him!" and went home. When she got back he was there, sitting with his feet up on the mantelpiece! She said, "Where were you?" He said, "Oh, well, one of the sheep wasn't well so I walked it back down to the farm." He hadn't bothered to come back to tell Hilda. She thought she could have been up there all night! She told him she wouldn't come with him any more, but she did. She told him she wouldn't drive him to the Downe Arms either. He said she'd have to, or he couldn't have a drink!

1961 Sunday School Trip to Saltburn. Hilda (rght) with daughters and Winsome Bonas

Tup Sales were held behind the Downe Arms. The tups would be fastened to door handles in Castleton High street, and the children were frightened to go out. Bessie said, "Pat Richardson was the auctioneer and he walked up the street selling. There were not many cars. If you got a dozen cars in Castleton it was a lot." Frank Farrow said. " I can remember when they used to bring them from all over on sheep sale day. The street was full of sheep, and there used to be loads of them coming up the village from different places, all being driven up at different times. Emma remembered that when they took the sheep to the show at Danby they walked them from Baysdale"

Village Policemen

Everyone agreed that the police didn't bother too much about drink and driving then, although Hilda had heard talk of one who had come in and had a drink with them, and then went out and put his uniform on to come back to catch them!

Derrick said they went "First Footing" one Christmas. The policeman who came with them was on duty. One of the first footers had the policeman's uniform on, another one his helmet ...

One of our policemen was a Mr Wright, a "bit of a character", who married a fisher lass from Whitby. Mr Alec Thompson was also remembered. He was a well-respected policeman who kept order amongst the lads with "a clip around the ear hole." Hilda remembered him chasing Herbert and the lads when they were young and he could catch them! The lads, including Hilda's Herbert, pushed Geordie Nicholson's car from where he lived near

One of the first cars in Castleton

the Fox down to the bottom of the road. Herbert had her mother's scarf on and he lost it. Mr Thompson came up to Hilda's house and said to her mother, "Is this your scarf?" "Yes." she said. "Thank you very much!" "You can't have it," said Mr Thompson. "It's evidence." But he never did anything more about it. Linda can remember Walter Coverdale telling her about how Mr Thompson used to hide, and try and catch the young men speeding by on their motorbikes. Derrick said all the lads had motorbikes. Policeman Mr Thompson lived in Church Street where Carol Evans lives now. He then moved to Westerdale Side. Policemen Mr Wright and Mr Buckton lived in the police house in Castleton too, and the cell is still in that house, with bars in the door. There was a policeman called Charlie Aldis, but he lived in the new police house that was built opposite the garage in more recent times.

Before he came to work here Mr Thompson was a mounted policeman at Stokesley. When he retired, for years he used to walk to Loftus every Friday for his pension. He was on duty at Stokesley Show one year and a policeman who was there gave him a lift back afterwards as far as Great Ayton but didn't bring him home, so he walked to Castleton from there.

Heroic "Bobby" Thompson makes a snow rescue, and "Sunlight Charlie"

One winter Mrs Lucy Fishpool from above the Quarries, a dress maker who was perhaps in her seventies at the time, had been to Middlesbrough to sew. When she caught the train home she got on the wrong one by mistake, and found herself in Brotton.   The bus from Brotton wasn't running Castleton way because of snow.

She tried to get Tom Bint to bring her home in his taxi, but they only got as far as Lockwood Beck. He said it was a waste of time trying to get further because they wouldn't get through the snow. She wouldn't be told, and she got out and set off to walk home. When he got home Tom Bint had the sense to telephone Mr Thompson, the Castleton policeman, and tell him what had happened. Also Mrs Fishpool's husband told the policeman he was worried that she hadn't come home.

Mr Thompson set off to look for her. Mr Fishpool went with him but had to turn back at White Cross because conditions were so bad. Mr Thompson went on. "He found that she hadn't got far from the Lockwood Beck turning, 4 miles from Castleton, before she'd fallen and couldn't get up again. Mr Thompson carried her on his back all the way home again to "Sunnybrow" in Castleton!"

Snow clearing, 1947

Derrick told about "Sunlight Charlie", who was Sylvia Watson's father. They lived at High Garth, and he used to own Sycamore Farm. There was a competition to find a name for a brand of soap, and Charlie wrote in suggesting "Sunlight Soap". It's still known today as Sunlight Soap, and Charlie won maybe £50 or £100 - a lot of money at the time - for naming it.

The Butcher's Story

When Frank Farrow left school at the age of fourteen he started work for Mr J. R. Watson at the butcher's shop in Danby on Saturdays, for 6d a day. He worked there for three years earning 7s 6d a week until in 1941 he was 17 and he went into the Army for five years. He began training at Plymouth, and he spent some time fighting in France and also in the desert.

Frank is the little boy in the centre, with parents Mary and Harold, and brothers Kenneth, left, and Leslie, right.

Frank keeps safe a newspaper photograph that he found after he was in France, because it is so exactly what he remembers of his experiences there. "I could have been one of those soldiers. It was just like that where I was. It was terrible." he said. He has photographs of various young men from the Parish who served in the war.

"Ray Beeforth was a rigger in the RAF," said Frank. "I met him during the war. I just ran into him on an airfield. Spitfires didn't go to a run way and take off at an expected time like planes do today. The airmen sat in the spitfires all the time and they got scrambled, red or yellow. They just popped their masks up, and off they went. When they came back if there were any bullet holes in those spitfires Ray put a patch on them. I saw him do it because I stayed two days on that airfield. Ray had a school master's blackboard outside the wooden huts the lads lived in, and every time a plane came back he asked what the airmen had done, maybe shot a train up, or shot an aircraft, and Ray chalked up whatever those lads had done. That blackboard would be something to have had a photo of!"

"They knitted scarves and other things here at home and sent them to us. I had some from them. Well, you see, you could only wear them in certain places. They where no good to you if you where in a camp, in proper uniform. You would only wear this clothing if you were living outside. If you slept out at night out in the fields or somewhere the clothing came in very useful then. I had some in the bottom of my kit bag."

Frank (2nd row from the front, the tall soldier near to the camera) aged 17, at training camp in Plymouth in 1941

"We used to go to a knitting group," Bessie said. "Mother used to knit white stockings for hospitals to use after operations; she did a lot of that." Hilda and Annie used to knit balaclavas. "We used to reckon to knit an ounce a night."

Frank's newspaper photograph of the war-time France that he remembers

Frank was given a "Welcome Home from the War" card which came with a gift of appreciation from the local committee, but he can't remember what the gift was.

When he came out of the army in 1946 meat was still rationed. For two years Frank went bus driving until the rationing stopped and then he went to work for a butcher in Ugthorpe. He spent 18 years there but he still helped the Danby butcher at night. After Mr Watson's death in 1968 he took over the shop. He retired in 1988 after more than 50 years in the trade.

Frank at army camp in the Desert

Frank's rounds were local when he first began delivering - Danby Dale and Westerdale - but then the farmers got their own freezers and started buying their stock back so he was forced to deliver further afield. He bought a van and covered Liverton Mines, Skinningrove, Loftus and Carlin How as well as his local round. He delivered to Grangetown and Eston. "I never missed a delivery there, "On two occasions I couldn't get home again because of the snow but I always got the meat delivered," he said.

"I used to go to the Unity Club in South bank on a Thursday night selling pies and meat, and I remember at the top of the stairs there was a one armed bandit machine. Two men came up and one says, "We are going to empty that machine, do you want to join in?" I said "No, I want nothing to do with you!" I could hardly speak I was that frightened! Anyway I just stood there and they got some wires out and they just pushed them in and they emptied the machine and then off they went. Right under my nose! Money came out - I saw it! On a different day, later, I was turning in to the street and there was six men carrying the same machine up the street, off with it! When I went to the club I saw they had cut the telephone wires. Upstairs there was dancing, and downstairs they had just taken the one armed bandit."

Frank's mother, Mary Farrow

Frank added, "I had a brand new van at the same period and it was parked in the street. There were three little lads and they started doing handstands on the van. So I thought, "What do I do?" I just said, "Bye, you're good lads! Do it again!" And do you know I had no bother with them three lads. They grew up and as they got older we had some respect. But if I'd gone at them – what then??"

"Just a bit of common sense," said Bessie

Frank said, "I never had my cash bag pinched off my back. I had stuff pinched from along side me. A pair of hands would come in and take five or six pies or pounds of sausage or a tray of bacon. But it was no good running down the street after them."

A story was told about "A fellow called Bainbridge who used to come over from Loftus with lemonade. He parked his wagon down at the Mill and little Georgy clipped a bottle of lemonade out of the back of the wagon. He didn't know that Mrs Bainbridge was sat in the front. He got his lug clipped for that."

The conversation turned to ploughing. When you ploughed a field wooden posts were put in for the ploughman to aim for to keep the furrows straight. Lester Pennock was ploughing a field when Johnny Cockerill and another fellow from Middlesbrough came along and they moved a wooden post. Lester came down the hill heading for the bit of stick and got it all wrong. Johnny and his friend were on the road watching.

"He would have a nice crooked field!" Bessie said.

"They were good fun days," said Frank.

Horses ready to work in 1951

A Troublesome Evacuee, Remedies and Food

Derrick recalled that his mother had an evacuee, a young lad who was always in trouble. "He was a devil. We had this stove going in the garage, and he was dripping drops of oil down onto the fire. Dad says to him, "That thing will be blowing up!" Of course little devil wouldn't take any notice and there was an explosion. He burnt all his hair and face and he ran out into Watson's field and sat up there. Mother had to go and retrieve him. She put a towel over his head and brought him back down. He said he would come back and see us when he was a skipper of his own boat, and he did come back."

Champions' Garage, Castleton

Betty Taylor told of some remedies. "You had a bottle of camphorated oil and soaked a sock in the oil and fastened it around your neck and you kept it there until your sore throat was better." Derrick said, "The lads who lived opposite the Blakey pub used to come to school with a pigs swath (strip of pig skin) round their necks." Betty said, "You used goose grease if you had a bad chest. A good way to stop getting a cold was to cut half an onion and put it in your pocket. My brother did this but didn't tell Mother until she got hold of his trousers. She couldn't bear the smell and felt in his pocket, and there was this rotten onion! A wart goes if you get hold of a snail and wipe it on. You have to leave it till the slime goes. And sulpher and treacle once a week got rid of spots." Frank commented, "It was nice to eat, I liked it!" Betty said, "I used to hate it, but you didn't get spots. On a Friday night you were given syrup of figs. We used carbolic soap for nits, dolly blue bags for bee stings, and boiled milk and ginger to warm you up. Sometimes we put bread in it. 'Pobs' we called it. And we used vinegar and paraffin to clean the windows and we never had any flies come in!"

"You ate what was put in front of you, and if you didn't eat everything you got no sweet after. "said Betty. "I wouldn't eat my rice pudding once, so I had to sit at the table until I did. All the others went out but I wasn't allowed and every meal time that rice pudding came out. When Dad walked past the table he tried to sneak a spoonful into my mouth but I wouldn't eat it. At breakfast they were all having bacon and eggs but that rice pudding came out again. I never ate it though, and Dad took it away in the end." Bessie said, "I loved tattie and onion pie. It usually had an egg cup in the middle to hold the pastry up if you didn't have enough filling." Everyone (almost) loved rabbit pie, and roast rabbit was served on Sunday to make the meat go further. Liver and onions, neck of mutton stew, pork dripping on bread with salt, lettuce with sugar and vinegar, and condensed milk on bread were much loved foods. "Scrapings" were made from pork fat. The fat was cut into squares and rendered down for lard and the crisp scrapings were a real treat. Betty said, "The house smelt awful after rendering days. I used to have to stir the blood after pig killing to stop it clotting, and then oatmeal, pearl barley and fat were added, I was only little when I had to do that." Frank Fishpool said, "You put eggs in water glass and you had hams hung up."

Frank Farrow said, "I remember a chap whose wife sent him to get a ham that was hung up high on the ceiling and when he lifted it down the sack was as light as could be. The ham had been fly blown and the maggots had eaten it all, only bone was left. I bet he got into trouble. They kept fine if you cured them right!!"

The Postmaster's Story

Allen Medd, a retired Castleton Postmaster now in his nineties, said that his family has lived in this area for generations. They lived at Prospect House and at various other places in and around Castleton village, including Dibble Bridge. His father was born in the eighteen hundreds, and the post office business in Castleton has been in the family probably since the mid nineteenth century. Allen's son has now sold the post office, ending generations of Medds in the Post Office trade in Castleton.

Allen Medd & his sister Mary – later Mary Armstrong

1960s Castleton. Old petrol pumps (left) by Champion's Garage Someone is unloading goods outside what is now "The Village Shop"
Postcard Judges of Hastings www.judges.co.uk

Allen said the Post Office has been in two or three different places. It's been next door to Campion House - that was too long ago for him to remember, and it was at "Wayside", and it was next door to the fruit shop (now the Village Shop). Allen's father bought the building where the present post office is, next to drive of the Downe Arms, after he came back from the army in about 1920. It had been a butcher's shop before the Watsons were butchers in the village. Allen's father took it over and he altered it.

At the front, where the Post Office bay window is now, there were two big double doors. Before the shop was altered the slaughter-house was at the back, where the kitchen is now. There was a "blood hole" there for when the cattle were slaughtered. Linda said that when she moved into "Apple Tree House", opposite "Montage", their kitchen floor sloped down to a drain and a blood hole. They levelled it all out. It had apparently been a slaughterhouse too, as were a few other houses in the village. Bessie said that people lived at "Apple Tree" house before Linda, and they didn't alter it. Linda said their kitchen must have sloped downhill!

Near the back entrance of the new 1920s post office was a small building where the cattle had been kept before they were slaughtered. From the back where the slaughter-house was there was probably another door, and Allen remembers two great wooden beams running from the back of the house to the front, where the slaughtered animals had been brought through into the butchers shop, hanging from a rail. His father had the two big beams taken out, and they were made into tongued and grooved boards from which the sitting room floor was made, by Harold Farrow, Frank Farrow's father. It was pitch pine. In the bedroom the ceiling was made of the pitch pine as well, and it's still there. Joseph Ford did some of the building, and Allen's Grandfather on his mother's side, John Dowey, did some of the work as well.

Allen said that all up one side of Castleton is built on sand. The sitting room floor was taken up and there was a tremendous hole dug to take sand out. Allen was only a young lad then but he remembers that Joseph Ford fell down the hole when he was walking backwards, looking up at Grandfather who was on a ladder! All the sand from under the floor was used for cementing the walls

T Watson WLPS

Old Castleton from below the sandy side of the ridge

On the plan in the deeds, before the post office was built in its present state, the building was called Slea House or Slea Cottage, and perhaps one or two little buildings had been on that particular site. The post office shop has a really good cellar that you get down into by a staircase. Allen's family used it as a coalhole, with a trap door at the front. Let into the wall at the back in the cellar is what looks as though it has been a window. It is made of dressed stone - what could it have been? There is another window exactly the same in the wall looking up the street - again beautifully made of dressed stone, but again, below ground level. Allen wonders if the cellar was there before the building above it.

Linda said she was told that three families lived at "Apple Tree" at one time. Hilda said that when she lived at Sycamore Farm her Dad told her that seven Quaker families had lived there. There was a tiny building that Hilda's family used as a hen house that was said to have been one of their dwelling houses.

When Allen's father was in the Great War his Aunts Sissy and Mary, and Arthur Watson looked after the Post Office. When the Post Office was at "Wayside" Allen's Grandfather kept a pony where there later was a saddler's shop, at the end of Wayside. Grandfather, Pickering Medd, was the Postman. There was no railway then up from Grosmont to Castleton. Pickering Medd used to go to Grosmont on a pony to pick up all the mail, and he delivered it all up the valley to Castleton. Perhaps this was once a week - Allen didn't know how frequently he would deliver mail.

When Allen was young and the post office was at Wayside, in the cottage end, he remembers that he used to just sit on a stool and watch. The little back room was used as a sorting office. They had a Morse code sounder there before there was a telephone in the village. Telegrams, which Allen aged 11 or 12 would often deliver, were received by Morse code.

Allen remembers, when he was 8 or 9, going up to his Uncle Martin's at Hill House at Westerdale and he borrowed an old road pushbike, without brakes or anything, from Jack Booth who was farming at Carr House in Westerdale. He learned to ride on it around the crossroads and down to Dibble and back round to Westerdale, and then he bought it for sixpence. His Aunty Ginny walked down towards Westerdale to meet him on his new bicycle, but it had a puncture, and Allen had to "push the ruddy thing home! I'd spent all that money and then had to push it!"

Grandfather's friend from Newcastle took a crystal set and pair of headphones and a long length of wire up to the Garth where Grandfather used to work. He rigged an aerial up and Allen listened to London on the crystal set. That was the first Allen knew about anything like that. When the telephone came to Castleton it was to the post office at Wayside in the early 1920s. Two telephone engineers installed it. They stayed in Castleton, and they built a large radio set during the time they were working on the telephones. Allen still has bits and pieces that they used in about 1920.

Allen said everybody has telephones now. Most people own a mobile phone and even children have them. Allen thinks that *everybody* except him has a telephone. He hasn't got one at all. When he and Dora were married in 1939 only about ten or a dozen people in the Castleton area had the telephone, and so the Medds took messages for people. They had a night and day telephone service, and if it rang during the night they had to get up and answer it. When he came out of the Navy in 1946 he vowed that he would never again have a telephone in his life, and he never has.

Allen went to Castleton School, he says "every so often." He then went to the Grammar School in Stokesley where his father used to go. One of the schoolmasters, Mr Jackson, lived in Castleton and he took Allen with him. He finished school at fourteen or fifteen and went into Castleton post office and he had to deliver telegrams and he learnt the post office trade.

When Allen started work a stamp cost a penny or a penny and a half. You could send a postcard for halfpenny. Now it's "three bob", Allen thought. Bessie said 32p. Over six shillings! Linda said ten shillings brought your groceries when she was first married.

Allen at Castleton School. He is top right, in front of the teacher.

41

When Father came out of the army he had an old belt-driven 1913 Triumph motorbike. Allen remembers going up to Farndale on the back of it, hanging on to Father's leather belt, to see Dick Shaw, the huntsman. They left the motorbike at the Blakey pub and walked across the railway line to Farndale Head. Allen gathered a bag of nuts while Father talked to Dick.

Allen remembers that in the mid 1920s his Father got a"Buckingham" car, owned originally by a chap who used to come and play for dances in Castleton. It was polished aluminium and Allen and his sister Mary sat in the little dicky seat at the back. It was a four-wheeler and it had an engine with two big cylinders stuck out in the air at the front.

A 1927 Wolsley Viper

Then in 1926 or 27 Father bought a new Wolsley four-seater car with a soft hood and celluloid side screens. It was new, but after a while the compensating overhead camshaft broke. Father contacted the Wolsley factory in Birmingham. He took it down there to the works and Allen went with him. Allen remembers seeing one of the earliest Wolsley cars in the foyer. After the mechanics had looked at their car and renewed the part of the engine that needed it they put it on the test track, which was a very steep ramp up the side of an enormous building and across the top and down the other side! Allen and his father stayed in Birmingham for maybe a day and a couple of nights and they went to a concert given by a violinist.

At that time Allen's father sold all sorts of things in the Post Office shop. He was interested in "push biking", and he sold various cycle parts. Allen had been nagging to his father about a new pushbike. He was now about nine or ten years old and had had to put up with the old one for a long time. Father said he would buy him a new one while they were in Birmingham. He did, but it was a box full of parts, and it wasn't built. It was all in pieces! Father said it would be Allen's first lesson in assembling and adjusting a pushbike. From then on Allen did a lot of biking. He delivered telegrams to Danby, Danby Dale, Danby Head, Gerrick, Commondale, Westerdale, Baysdale and so on. He remembers that during shooting time he often had to cycle over a sheep track to Baysdale three or four times in a day, all for one shilling and sixpence, for people sending and receiving telegrams. He escaped getting shot!

The Council would have been responsible for the roads, and in Castleton there used to be a couple of roadsmen who cleaned the roads, clearing them of horse muck and so on, and they cleared the gutters. One was an old chap called Underwood (no relation to Bessie), and George Husband was another. Later on George had a cobbler's shop in the garden that Ted Williamson has now. Hilda remembers old Mr Atkinson, who was a roadsman and also had a barber's shop. Near the station there were two big heaps of flints, and Mr Atkinson, who was lame, used to sit down with a hammer and break the flints up into small pieces for mending the road. At his barber shop he would do shaving and haircutting, and Allen could get his hair cut then for sixpence.

The unmetalled road over the bridge at Castleton

Even the village roads in those days were just sand, mud and stone - there was no tarmac even through Castleton. A water cart, roller and steamroller came through occasionally. There were spikes on the back wheels of the roller that tore up the roadway. Then it was re-layed and sprayed with water then rolled flat with the steamroller. That was how the road was all the way across the Rig to Hutton-le-Hole. Motoring was quite an adventure, and there was not much traffic on the road then.

Hilda remembers that she once delivered telegrams for Mr Clemments for sixpence, from Danby up to Danby Dale. She remembers going to Low Coombes there to deliver two telegrams because there was a wedding. She was thrilled to bits because she saw it. Bessie said that when she was married they got fourteen telegrams, and she still has them. Emma Skidmore said she got one, and still has it. Bessie said that Alan Medd himself must have delivered theirs to New Hall. They weren't the fancy ones that came later. They were just plain yellow. Hilda had a fancy one from her Aunty in Leeds for her wedding. There are no telegrams received now.

Mr & Mrs Martin Helm. A Westerdale wedding in 1931. This is Emma Skidmore's Aunt Ethel, married from Bagdale.

Bessie said sometimes her husband, postman Reg, "was reported". He had to go two or three times to the office at Scarborough because he had done something "wrong". That was when he did little jobs for the elderly people living around Westerdale, and he wasn't supposed to do that. Hannah Mary Carr was one person that he helped, and Mrs Hardy's folk, the Lumbs. Then he was reported for giving Mrs Dennier a ride in his van. This was by a chap who could walk, but who wanted a ride. Reg had told him he couldn't give him a ride because he wasn't allowed to. In Scarborough Reg was told he might lose his job. He said to his boss, "Well could *you* possibly see an old lady of ninety-two walking? Could *you* possibly see an elderly person stuck? I shall still do it!" They never did anything to him - he just had to go and report. He wasn't gaining anything for himself. He was just doing a good turn! Everybody did that then, they looked after their neighbours.

43

Race Cards, the Tin Church, and the "Toilet Position"

Alan Medd, who is in his nineties, said that in the early days when there was an election for the Parish Council, local people made for everyone what they called a "Race Card", and the various councillors were given different names.

The Danby
Parochial   Point-to-Point

FOR HORSES OF ANY AGE OR SEX.

RUN ON ALL FOOLS DAY, 1946.

HORSES	TRAINER	JOCKEY
Dr. Nansen	Tarmac	Shunter
Sacred Melody	Barry	Pie Centre
Reporter	Little John	Clerk of Works
Bury Ambition	Bantam	Early Bird
Second Choice	Evacuee	Linthorpe Lass
Scholastic	High Jump	Poor House
Laughing Cavalier	Poverty	Dribble
Prophet	Nervous	Come To-morrow
Gated Rd. Arab	Large White	Undertaker
Dalesman	Sound Sleeper	High Burrows
Institute Lass	Keyboard	Saltburn Sands
Genevieve	Berkshire	Absolute Fallacy
Pongo	Divinity	Canteen

PONGO—Brown Colt, 3 years, 17.3 h.h. A big, headstrong colt and very wild. Ran well in the Last Ditch Stakes, but was badly beaten in Eskdale Cue Handicap. His trainer is far too quiet to handle a horse like this, and he may give the starter some trouble. Is ridden by a lady who will be lucky if she does not part company with her mount. He will run in blinkers, and although a long way down in the prices may be a surprise packet. His trial was witnessed by In Loving Memory, By Jove Yes, Tomato, Resting, Rudyard, CON.F.S., Mother McRea, Perky, Ricksy, Superintendent, Royal Mail, and M. & C.

BY CHANTICLEER.

Extracts from the Parish Council Election "Race Card" for 1946

Allen's father was "Laminay". There were leaflets with the names on - Emma has copies of two different ones. Some of the names were quite cheeky - it's perhaps as well that their proper names aren't known, though Hilda remembers that Mr Wright the school teacher was called "Pongo", and that became his nickname. He used to teach Hilda, and he used to referee football matches when Allen played.

Allen spoke about attending the "Tin Church" in Castleton before the new one was built eighty years ago. Emma pointed out that there are few people still alive who remember that. He said that there was a little tin porch, and inside there were normal wooden pews. In the middle of the church was a pot-bellied stove to warm the church. When it was harvest time and on special occasions it was full. Allen used to sit in the choir stalls near the altar. It was

Castleton "Tin Church" viewed from Ashfields

noisy when there was a hailstorm! Everyone agreed that the tin church must have been built because it cost little to do, and was quick to put up. It would have been a long walk to go to Danby Church.

Down in Ashfield a long time ago there was a mill and the water was brought to it in an open drain from Mill Woods. There once had been a row of cottages in the field near the road going up from the river. There's no evidence now of any buildings in the field except for the side by the Ashfield bridge. There is evidence there of a number of stone steps up into the field where the cottages were. Bessie said she has heard about there being a linen mill down there, where they used to wash and treat the linen.

Allen remembered the early days when the Show was in the field behind the Downe Arms where the Bowling Green is now. There was even a band - Castleton's own! Emma's husband Allen Skidmore's Grandad, John Medd, played in the band. He was killed working at Commondale brickworks at the age of 29. Allen still has a tobacco jar he made there.

At another time in the year there used to be a "Tup Fair", and all the tups were tied up in Castleton village. There were sheep sales too.

Castleton Band in 1908-09. Amongst the players are
John Medd, Nathan Medd & Harry Clemmit.

45

Allen said that when he was eight or nine years old, in the early days, there were very few water toilets. In Bakers Yard before it was altered all the houses had "netties" up at the top of their gardens, and when Allen and his friends were lads they used to go up to the gardens there. At one phase of the "toilet position" as he called it, there was a soil cart, drawn by one horse, that used to come around during the night and empty the earth closets. Allen said it would be a community service that very few people knew about. He thought Walter Booth at Carr House was one who did it, and possibly Fred Watson and Sedman Featherstone might have been others. They were known as the " Ket Men", ket meaning 'rubbish'. Some called them "The Midnight Angels".

Pam who is in her sixties and is an "incomer" of over twenty years to Bagdale in Westerdale, couldn't imagine why double or treble sitters were built. Who would want to go to the toilet in company? Emma Skidmore said that children who had them were glad of double sitters on really dark nights. They only dared go across together, with a stable lamp.   Connie, who lived at Felixkirk when she was a child, said that to get to their toilet they came out of their back door and across some flags and round the corner. On rainy nights there were worms crawling along the flags. So she used to come out armed with a salt sprinkler and sprinkle all the worms to get rid of them. They would shrivel up immediately. She still hates worms! Connie remembers the Ket Men coming with big

Westerdale School Toilets - back to back, girls' and boys'.

buckets. By then they had a motor vehicle, and Emma remembers a ket vehicle coming to Westerdale. Hilda also remembers seeing Ket Men. They had deep "tub" carts, she thinks. The men spread the contents on the farmers' fields.

Hilda said at Danby School the toilets, or 'netties', had a door in at the back into the field behind, and the lads used to get nettles and nettle people's bottoms! Emma said they did at Westerdale School too. The toilets, girls' and boys', were back to back there.

In Linda's time at Dale Side in Westerdale the toilet was just emptied onto the midden. Connie said theirs was too. On farms nobody bothered to come and empty them very often. Bessie said it was a horrid job for somebody to do - nobody liked doing it. Connie said there was an ash pit further away from their house, and if the nettie got a bit full before the men came to empty it her father would empty it in there. There weren't just her family using it but also evacuees, during the war, so they needed a bit more space. Bessie remembered how they cut newspapers into squares and threaded them on a string and hung them on the door to use for toilet paper. It was no good using shiny papers.

Allen compared the ease today with which we do all these things - he used to have a bath in front of the fire!

Allen Medd, his wife Dora (nee Duck) and son David

Divisions

When he was a schoolboy Allen Medd had music lessons in one of the rooms above what is now the "Montage Art Gallery " on Castleton High Street. It belonged to a painter and decorator, Mr Meggison, and there were two Miss Meggisons, Winnie and Bessie. Winnie was a teacher and she gave Allen music lessons. Not for very long, because Allen played a lot of cricket and football so didn't do much piano practice. He learned music, but couldn't play properly and often got his knuckles rapped.

Linda said Miss Meggison might have rapped Allen's knuckles when she was younger, but Linda remembers her as a sweet old lady who taught her at Chapel Sunday School. Bessie said she taught her boys, too, at Sunday school. She thought Miss Meggison was a very good teacher, although she was strict then.

In the early days, Allen said, when the Meggisons and the Knaggs lived in Castleton and Tom Knaggs was the blacksmith he used to make the children a steel hoop, to bowl with a stick along the road. It was a good game to race the hoops. He has an idea there is still one left in the cellar at the present Post Office.

The Blacksmith's shop around 1916

Allen said that in those early days when he went for music lessons, and even later until quite recently, there was much "bias" between the Chapel people and the Church people. None of them would entertain the idea of any of the others going into their Chapel or Church during a service. Old George Meggison and Tom Knaggs would never entertain anyone from the Church going into the Chapel, or any of their own Chapel folk going to the Church. Allen thinks that bias is one reason why his Grandfather on his father's side changed from being a Wesleyan. He did a lot of work on the new Church when the Liddles were building it. Until a few years ago in Danby and Castleton the Wesleyan Parson would *never* come and deliver a service in the Church, and alternatively the same. Now people are much more broadminded, and there is a better attitude, and Chapel and Church folk get together.

Connie Watson agreed, and she remembers that when she first came to live here from Felixkirk, there had been a terrific divide between Church and Chapel. Connie was brought up "Church of England", but when she came here she began going to Chapel and she really enjoyed the singing. She didn't mind whether she went to Church or Chapel when she got here , but between Felixkirk Church and Sutton Chapel there was a big divide.

When she came to live here, Connie used to go with Mrs Watson to chapel, because her husband Fred would drive her there but then he wouldn't go in with her. If he went anywhere, he would run across the fields to Danby Church. Connie can't think how they ever got married, because one of them was Chapel and one was Church. They did get married, at Commondale Chapel. Chapel people have to be buried at the Church in the end, though, because the only Chapel burial ground in the area is at Glaisdale. As Pam said, you all go to the same place in the end.

Danby Church

There always was a big divide, not only between Church and Chapel, but also between children living in Danby and Castleton. Hilda said that as children when they lived at Danby, if they came to Castleton Chapel the Castleton children used to throw stones at them. Danby children and Castleton children just didn't mix - even between the two churches. Everyone agreed that things have greatly improved nowadays.

The Quakers & Dibble Bridge

Allen asked if anyone could remember the Quaker Meeting House in Castleton. Nobody could, though Frank Fishpool has a photograph of his brother when he was a child during the war, and the Quaker Meeting House is beyond him in the photo. It was at the end of Castleton Parish Rooms, where the electricity sub-station now is. It was HQ for the Home Guard during the war. There is a Quaker burial ground higher up in Castleton, well above the Moorlands on the same side of the road. There was a Meeting House and a Quaker school at Great Ayton.

Allen remembers the Quakers in this area being very "neutral", not minding whether people were Church or Chapel. He doesn't remember how often they held their meetings in their Meeting House. One of the main Quaker families of the time was the Pumphreys at Thornaby, who were in the confectionary trade. They had a house here at the top of Langburn Bank. There was another family who were confectioners at Stockton, and they had a house at Sunnybrow and went to work at Stockton. Long ago there were Quaker weavers living at remote St Helena towards the head of Danby Dale.

Frank Fishpool's brother Robert with the old Castleton Meeting House

Bessie remembers later a Mrs Richards at Fairbanks, who was a Quaker. She had a pram shop in Linthorpe Road in Middlesbrough, where Emma bought a "proper pram"! Mrs Richards sometimes held a Toy Fair in Castleton Village Hall at Christmas and once or twice she held it at Margaret Wilson's on the top road. Linda remembers coming from Westerdale to that. Bessie still exchanges letters each year with Mrs Richard's daughter.

Allen thinks the Castleton Meeting House closed because eventually there was "such a "collection" of Quakers at Darlington". They used to come up to Castleton occasionally, but the numbers attending the Meeting House dwindled down, and then the building was sold. Allen said, "Watson bought it." Emma Skidmore remembered that the stone from the Meeting House was used to build an extension to the house at Dibble Bridge. She was living at the bungalow there and working in the house at the time when they built it. The builders were called Carruthers, from Whitby, and they travelled up on the train to work every day. It was a really hot summer, and Emma remembers that one poor man stood in the yard near the stable in the heat every day and dressed the stone.

The Liddel brothers

Allen remembers the Liddel brothers who built the church. One was a stonemason who worked in a tin shed at the back of the new Castleton Church dressing the stone that was used to build it. Mr Weatherill worked at the old quarry at Westerdale side, cutting stone for the new Castleton Church. Derrick said Tommy Boyes led the stone up for the new church. Emma has a little book with the initials in of those who worked on it. Fred Watson was one. They found some water at the bottom end of the site when they were building and got the architect to come to see it. He said just to carry on. There's a damp spot there even now! The Garth at the bottom end is damp too.

Allen said that a professional landscape gardener designed the gardens and rockery at Dibble Bridge House for Captain Cruise, who was in the army. At one time Allen's father bought Dibble Bridge together with thirty acres of land, and lived there.

Work

Bessie and Elsie said that they began work as soon as they could sit on a stool to milk a cow. That was one of the first jobs they did, as well as feeding the calves and the poultry and collecting eggs ... putting a hand under "a clocker", which would peck at you. Bessie remembers putting hens to sleep! She would tuck a hen's head under its wing, hold it in her arms and then "spin round and round for ever so long". She would then set the hen on the floor and it would stay there. Bessie and her brother would see how many hens they could set in a line before the first one woke up. Bessie said it was good fun to see how long they would stay asleep. Elsie said she wondered whether the hens thought it was fun! Bessie thought they were all right, because they didn't lay any better or worse, and Elsie said sometimes it was a useful way to get them to sit on eggs. Bessie said that as children they didn't really need toys - they had animals! They would put a cat in the dolls' pram and cover it over and wheel it round and round and see how long it would stay there. Linda used to dress her kittens up in dolls clothes.

Elsie in 1931

Elsie said she only had one job, and that was "Hard Work"! She milked before she went to school. Bessie's family had about six cows. Elsie thinks her family had about a dozen. It was a nice warm job hand milking cows in the winter, in the cow byre. Then in summer it was all flies.

When Bessie left school she helped at home a lot, but she also went out to lots of houses to do housework. "I biked four miles to Lealholm on Tuesday mornings to a farm where they had three little kiddies. I had to be there at seven thirty in the morning and I worked until ten at night and then went to bed. I got up the next morning, did another full day's work, and then biked home." She was paid two shillings and sixpence a day. "So that was five shillings, or today twenty-five pence, for two solid days' work! I thought nothing of it then - that was my wages." She worked on her family's farm at Broadgate in Westerdale too but not for a wage. Bessie said farming didn't pay girls. It paid for her brothers, who all had a wage, but she never did. She was given her food and then could keep whatever she earned when she went out working elsewhere, to buy her clothes and pay for a "Sixpenny Dance" whenever she wanted to go.

Elsie used to go to a neighbouring house to do the washing, and would also churn butter. She also used to go to Ainthorpe where her Grandma and Grandad lived, to help them. She used to go for a day, stay overnight and come back the next day and they used to pay her half a crown. Bessie's Grandparents did the same for her when she worked for them.

At thirteen and a half Emma Skidmore worked in the school holidays and at weekends for Teddy Watson at Dibble Bridge House, and at fourteen she began work there full-time. She worked there for seven years, until he sold Dibble Bridge House.

Linda said she did the same at thirteen years old, working in the holidays and at weekends at Dibble Bridge House for Lady Gisborough. Linda ironed Lady Gisborough's sheets. She had to have clean sheets on her bed every day. In a room across the yard there was a large table and Linda had to put each sheet on the table and iron it without a crease, and then get the sheet, still uncreased, onto the bed. Lady Gisborough just didn't have creases in her bed linen! Linda said it was a difficult thing to do - especially when the geese chased her. She was glad she was only there for the summer holidays!

Emma Skidmore's job at one time was to look after two children at Dibble Bridge, and she was paid ten shillings a week. Then she moved on to be the cook at Kildale Hall. She said she just got her cookery book out, and "did it!" "Old Mrs "Granny" Turton at Kildale Hall

Early years - Thompson family. Emma (Skidmore), Joe & Bill are standing, Mary in her father's arms and Michael in his mother's.

was absolutely lovely. She was 'eighty something' when I worked for her." Emma also worked for sixteen years at Ellerstang for Miss Punch, and it was interesting work and she enjoyed it. Bessie worked for a long time too at the Downe Arms, and she worked at Beddows, and for Miss Muddle who was a teacher in a private school in Middlesbrough.

Bessie worked for Mary Jane Thompson down at Ashfield in Castleton at the time that Mary had a cycling club visiting each week for teas. Bessie worked for many

households, all in this area, because when her husband Reg started work for the Post Office his wages dropped from twenty pounds a week to only eight pounds a week, although he had a very good pension scheme. They were looking ahead because of the pension scheme, which benefited them in the end to a certain extent. So Bessie had to go out to work. Reg enjoyed his job, being a postman, and working at the local garage. (Emma said she and Alan only had five pounds a week when they were married.)

Bessie's husband Reg Underwood (back 2nd left) in Castleton football team, 1947

Hilda's first job was for only a year, doing housework for a Miss Smith. Bessie said that after that Hilda worked at home and has been working hard ever since! Hilda agreed. Hilda remembers when she was young there was a Mr Harold Parkinson, who once asked her, "Are you going to the shop?" When Hilda said she was, Mr Parkinson asked her, "Will you get me some sweets? I want a quarter of round squares." She puzzled all the way to Castleton - it sounded odd. She went in and asked Mr Verrill for them. He just laughed, and said, "Tell Mr Parkinson I'll see him!"

Bessie was born in Hole House in Fryup. When Bessie was about seven or eight and she lived at Lieth House in Westerdale she did a Saturday job washing the floor in a

long stone passage for her mother. Mr Will Atkinson used to come in with the groceries every month. When he saw her scrubbing the floor he would always say, "Oh, thoo poor little thing! Here thoo is," and he gave her a halfpenny every month because whenever he came she was always doing the same job.

Bessie was the same age as his daughter, but his daughter never had to wash kitchen floors! Bessie can still hear his voice. Elsie said they used to wash their big kitchen floor, and then scrub

Mr Will Atkinson from the British Colonial Stores (now the Co-op) in Castleton

and whiten it round the edges. It was done once a week. There were clip mats laid on it. It was all hard work for housewives - washing, baking, doing the bedrooms, baking again, black-leading the fireplaces, and cleaning up, and then going to church two or three times on Sunday. On washday Monday it was a race to see who could get the washing out first in the morning. They would look round at the other farms. "So and so has got their whites out!" The whites all needed boiling.

When she was a small child, before she moved to Westerdale, Emma Beeforth who is now 84 lived in Castleton up the road from the Moorlands Hotel in the second cottage before the blacksmith's house. The blacksmith was her uncle. Emma remembers going to Mr Knagg's blacksmith shop, and the smell of the burning hooves of the horses. He was the only blacksmith in the village, and he was Barry Knagg's father.

Emma Beeforth's first job was in 1937 at Miss Leonard's Boarding House, in Ainthorpe. Then in 1938 she went to work for the Bonas family at Hall Farm at Westerdale. Bessie remembers passing on her way to school and seeing Emma there then. Emma didn't live in. She did housework, and all sorts of other work for Hall Farm. The stone flagged floors that had to be cleaned were hard work, laid throughout the kitchen and right to the far end of the cow byre. She earned £1 a day. Bessie earned fifteen shillings a day when she worked four days a week at the Downe Arms in Castleton, and she thought she was well off. The Bonuses didn't make butter - they sold the milk on. When she was young Bessie used to walk with her mother to shop at Castleton, and on the way back they used to stop to have a cup of tea at Hall Farm with Mrs Bonas and she remembers Mary, a little girl at the Bonases born in 1933, who liked "sugar sandwiches" - bread and butter with sugar on.

A lot of men worked at Castleton quarry. There was also a quarry at Westerdale. Linda talked about Mrs Dale, who said that her husband went out of the village to work at the mine in Lingdale, and Linda thinks he was killed at the mine. Elsie said that Nora Booth's husband was killed there too, and also Mrs Armstrong's husband, and they hadn't been married for long.

Bessie said that some men did leave the village to work. In earlier days they would walk to Blakey Rigg to build the railway line to Battersby. Bessie's husband Reg worked for the Water Board when they built Scaling Dam, for all the time that it was being built. There was a brick works at Commondale that closed in the 1950s. There wasn't only farm work to be done.

Mr Weatherill at Castleton Quarry

52

Rabbits, fish and chips and medals

Bessie said that she and Reg had an old blacksmith's shop for a garage when they came to live in Castleton. Frank Duck had owned it, and then the Graingers bought it and they rented it to Reg and Bessie for years. One half they used as a garage and in the other half Reg and their son Robert bred rabbits for a man called Cook, out Bilsdale way. The rabbits were sold to eat. Bessie cleaned the rabbit cages out and she didn't like the job. She got fed up, and the rabbits had to go in the end.

Emma Beeforth's husband Sid came from Danby. They met at a dance. People didn't go far to meet people. Elsie said, "In Castleton on a Saturday night - we hadn't far to go for our entertainment!" Emma added, "Fish van at the corner!" In the early 1940s a fish and chip van operated by Matty Pearson came to Castleton on a Saturday night. Young people from the villages walked to Castleton to get fish and chips and then walked back.

Emma said that just last Monday David and Betty Hartley visited her, bringing a lady and gentleman to see her who were looking for information about a man named George Frank. Elsie and Emma remembered George Frank at whist drives. They were frightened in case he came to their table because he always knew exactly what cards were in their hands!

The lady who visited had with her a war medal that was given "from the Parish and the community to George Frank of Westerdale Parish". She would like to give it back to the Frank family. She buys and sells items at auctions, and found the medal in a box of things that were turned out from a house in Glaisdale. She has the written history of the medal. Emma Skidmore said sadly that she has lost her Dad's medal. After he died she had the medal put on a chain, and thought, "I'm going to wear it." But the very first time she wore it she lost it. She searched all the places she'd been in, but didn't find it.

DANBY PARISH WELCOME HOME FUND.

The Committee hereby offer you a real Welcome to your home Village, and heartiest congratulations on your safe return from loyal and devoted service to your King and Country.

You are asked to accept the accompanying gift as some small token of the affectionate regard for you by the willing subscribers to this Fund.

Best wishes to you for your future success and happiness.

Danby, April 20th, 1946.

Given to Frank Farrow on his return from the War

Bessie talked about her Grandmothers' candlesticks that had belonged to two different Grandmas, on each side of the family. After they each died someone in the family in both cases couldn't decide who should have them, and gave one of the set to Bessie. So she ended up with a pair that didn't match, one from each Grandma! Someone else must have an odd pair too.

Living in Egton in the 1930s

Dorothy Dowey who in 2007 is 77, has lived in Westerdale since she was married. She left school at Egton in the Esk Valley in the December that she was fourteen, as her head teacher retired and a new one arrived. The new head teacher taught Dorothy for just the last fortnight of her time at school. Dorothy helped at home for a while, but then the new head teacher came to see Dorothy's mother to ask if she could spare Dorothy to come and look after her daughter who was just a year old. That was Dorothy's first job and

Dorothy in 2007

she started work at Easter, looking after the little girl at School House. She worked there until the little one was old enough to go to school. Dorothy didn't live in. She started work at 8.30am, and then left at 4pm when the teacher came home. The head teacher and her family eventually left to go to live at Chipping Camden, and so Dorothy's job ended. She was asked straight away to do another job elsewhere and that happened each time she had to leave a job so she never had to ask for work. She left the last job to get married. Then she worked on the farm and looked after her husband, the house and the children.

Dorothy said, "One job I had to do when I was young was leading cart horses out. I remember my father setting me off, warning me not to get my feet trodden on by the horses". Bessie said her big toe is still peculiar because her foot was trodden on by a horse! Emma Beeforth said their old pony Toby did the same to her when she took him to the water trough at Westerdale.

Dorothy's mum came to Yorkshire from Staffordshire for a holiday with her aunty and uncle when she was sixteen. "While she was here she liked Yorkshire and got a job, so she stayed." When her parents first met her father was living on a farm that adjoined her Grandad's smallholding.   Dorothy's father then got a job in the steelworks at Grangetown. Her Mum then worked in Hintons grocers shop in Middlesbrough. They gave up their jobs when they married and came to live at Egton where her 'Grandad' (really he was her mother's uncle) had a market garden along Aislaby Side. He had a flat cart to take the vegetables to a shop in Whitby and Dorothy remembers going with him. He was a local preacher. When Dorothy's parents were married and came to live at Egton her father bought a little smallholding which had two cottages on it and her parents lived in one of the cottages, with her father's family farm nearby.

Scarlet Fever

Bessie spoke about an epidemic of scarlet fever in the area in the late 1920s or early '30s when she was a child. She said, "My Grandparents lived at the Lodge up at Botton Hall in Danby Dale, when a family lived in the big house.

Botton Hall in Danby Dale

Grandma was the cook there, and Grandad was a gamekeeper. When scarlet fever was pretty rife Grandma took in John and Dorothy Rudsdale and Frances Cockerill because Mrs Rudsdale had scarlet fever and I think she went into hospital. Dorothy was just a baby. Grandma got the sack from the family at Botton Hall, because she'd taken the three children in, and they said she could have brought the disease in to them." Bessie's Grandparents had to move out of the Lodge. "I can remember it because Mum and Dad had to take Grandma and Grandad in, because they were homeless. It was all through doing a good turn!" Annie said that when she was born her mother got the sack from the family at Botton Hall, because she'd had a baby. That was the way things were in those days. She doesn't know how her mother would have managed, with two children to bring up. Then when Annie got to her teens the family there relied on her! She worked for them three days a week, for seven shillings and sixpence. They used Botton Hall as a holiday home.

Emma Skidmore remembered that Frances Cockerill got scarlet fever and Frances has talked about how she was taken in a pony trap to the isolation hospital at Guisborough. Emma's husband to be, Alan, had it too. It was a dangerous disease then. Annie said that she also had scarlet fever, and she was only three years old at the time. She also had to go to the isolation hospital. She remembers her mother looking through the window at her in the hospital, but she couldn't come in. Annie said, "I was given a lot of presents, but they wouldn't let me bring them home!" She and her brother Les were taken there together, with scarlet fever. "The Dowsons had it first, then we did, and then the Rudsdales." Derrick Champion remembers Keith Rudsdale being taken in a horse ambulance to Guisborough. Annie said she doesn't remember what she travelled in, but it would have been at the same time, to the same place. Hilda remembers that there was another outbreak in later years. John Scarth and his wife who ran the village shop in Castleton lost their little boy, Alan, who was four years old. Because it was scarlet fever they had to take everything out of their shop and burn it.

The Village Doctors

A doctor who worked in the valley from the 1920s until the 1940s was remembered. He was a kind doctor. He did enjoy a drink. Annie remembers that when she was a child the family were in bed one night. Her father was out, and the door was locked. The doctor came to their house in mistake for another farm further away where a woman was having a baby. He came in and went upstairs to her mother's bedroom. "We were able to re-direct him."

Reg Gaines, Annie's father, with one of his cart horses

Derrick Champion's mother, Adelaide, when a young woman

Emma Skidmore said her brother Michael was the first baby to be delivered in the area by Nurse Phillips. Emma said Nurse Phillips had two leaving presentations, because she left, and then came back again. Ivy Layton came to work in the surgery, dealing with the medicines. She was buried at Danby. Emma said, "Ivy Layton held me when I got my thumb out of joint so the doctor could put it back!"

Derrick remembers, when they were living at the Mill, falling off a motorbike when he was only about eleven or twelve years old. It was in Ashfield. He shouted and shouted, and little Jeremy Williamson came up. The Williamsons had some visitors with them including a nanny who came to help Derrick too. They pulled the motorbike off him, and they walked him down to his home at the Mill. He can remember Jeremy saying, "Are you all right?" but his arm was hanging off!

They fetched the doctor and he chased Derrick around the table until he caught him, then he dabbed the arm with iodine and wrapped it up with tape. The tape was on for a week or ten days, and then Derrick said to his Mum, "My arm's starting to smell." His mother took the tape off with difficulty, "but when she got some of it off we could see the bones working - it was rotten!" His mother took the nursing over then. "You can still see where the rotten part was because there is a lump missing." Everyone agreed that that doctor liked to put sticky tape on everything.

Derrick said that when he was called up he had to go to Middlesbrough for a medical. When he saw Derrick's arm the medic asked, "Who treated that?"

Bessie remembers that her son Lesley cut his arm badly on some rusty tin sheeting. She said he should go to the doctor for a tetanus injection, but he said, "I don't want to go to the doctor!" So she covered it with iodine and put a bandage on. The next day she took the bandage off, and he had a huge blister from the iodine! But he didn't get tetanus. He still has the scar, and says he can still feel that iodine. Bessie said she didn't know you shouldn't cover iodine. They wondered if that's what went wrong with Derrick's arm. Derrick said he showed it to another doctor when he was visiting Westerdale one day. That doctor came from Sleights, where he lived. Derrick's arm kept "locking". He suggested an x-ray, and when the result came back he told Derrick, "There's more gravel in thy arm than there is in Westerdale Road!"

The village doctor always had a bottle of medicine handy that he had made himself, probably with liquorice in. Bessie said he cut her hair short once when she was a small child, because she had a very gluey ear and was deaf. She remembers sitting on his knee, and he had a watch. He said, "Can you hear it?" It got right down really close to her before she said," Yes." She had curly hair, and he said she would be better without it. She was too young to mind about her hair. They remembered him always having his trilby hat, and putting it on the table with his gloves inside it when he visited. At dances he always wore white gloves.

Dr Jack Alexander was mentioned. He rode on a horse over to Rosedale to treat patients there. Derrick remembered how he was the first to get to the bus that got stuck in the snow for three days near Fat Betty at the head of Rosedale in 1933. Hilda remembers seeing Dr Jack on his horse. He wasn't married, but he lived with his three sisters and they had a farm near Old Man's Park where Miss Punch used to go for all her milk and cream.

The story of a Man who had an Accident

Derrick told a story about Gerald, who was "a bit of a Bandy Boy". Derrick was driving one night with his brother in law to pick one of the Mead lads up from Loftus and they passed Gerald walking towards Danby. Derrick said to his brother in law that they would pick Gerald up as they came back. But when they returned Gerald was lying in the gutter by Six Arch Bridge. "There were people there picking him up when we pulled up. One lad stayed with him, and the other came along with me in the taxi to the police house - Alec Thompson was the policeman then. I took him back to Gerald." The policeman asked him to go with him to take Gerald to the doctor. "The doctor said to take him to hospital. The doctor's assistant, Ivy Layton said that Gerald had been on fire, but he didn't smoke! The back of his coat was burnt and brown. It was from being dragged by a car along the road.

"When Gerald was taken into hospital he was laid out unconscious on a table. It was the name of Nurse Jennifer Cowan from Baker's Yard in Castleton that revived him. She was a bonny lass. When he heard her name he called, "Jennifer!" Nurse Jennifer kept an eye on him in the hospital. Her dad used to be the postman at one time. Gerald was in such a bad state

The accident happened behind the trees before the road goes on to Castleton, left centre top. He was found half a mile on from the brow of the hill. Notice Tin Pan Alley, bottom right corner. Postcard Judges of Hastings www.judges.co.uk

with his back burnt and a big hole in the back of his head." Hilda said it was amazing he came round. Derrick said, "He was as tight as a tick though, and wouldn't have felt anything." They left him in the Whitby hospital corridor. They thought he wouldn't live the night out.

Gerald's coat had been caught by something on a car and he had been dragged from near Stang End, over two bridges and around the corner as far as Howe Farm. It was a really frosty night. "When we came home we pulled up where he'd been knocked down and we picked up car bits, and pieces of his scarf and so on. People said, "He's never been dragged as far as that!" but the evidence was there - we could see the marks in the frost where he had been knocked down and then dragged."

People were in church at early communion when they got back, and Derrick went around all the cars that were in the car park and had a good look. Alec Thompson asked Derrick to tell him if he heard anything, and Derrick kept finding people who had seen Gerald. But then the enquiries just went dead.

Gerald recovered, and lived a long life. Derrick thinks whoever it was who had knocked him down "paid out" to Gerald. He certainly came into a bit of money round about then, and he began to hire taxis to take him out, and he sometimes went to the theatre at Middlesbrough. He used to "do the job right", Derrick said, and even had a box at the theatre. Derrick's father used to take him in the taxi most times, and his father went to sit with a man who ran a picture house nearby until the theatre finished and then he picked Gerald up and brought him home.

Westerdale Vicarage, which used to stand in the church yard until it was demolished "because of damp".

Gerald was a postman for a long time - he was when Bessie's husband Reg joined the Post Office. He had a bike but he didn't ride it. "He took it into Hardisty's field on the corner in Westerdale, practicing, but he just couldn't ride it. He couldn't!" So Gerald put the postbag on the bike and just pushed it. He abandoned the bicycle in the end. A lot of undelivered post was found in Gerald's room. They were mainly circulars, but Hilda said that someone up at Woodend knew that a birthday card had been sent and it should have arrived. They reported it and Alan Medd sent Gerald all the way back up to Woodend to deliver it.

For a while Gerald lived at the Westerdale Vicarage with Mr Jones the vicar and his wife, because no one else would have him. Emma Beeforth said, "It wasn't a very good arrangement. Gerald used to cook in his bedroom - I remember because I used to work a little for Mr and Mrs Jones. I remember Mr and Mrs Jones once being about to go out when Gerald rushed in, saying, "I'm ready, Vicar, I'm ready!" He wanted to go out with them. Then he lived in Castleton."

Hilda said, "And Gerald ended up with nothing." They all agreed. Bessie said he had cardboard in his shoes - it was terrible. Derrick said that many a time when he was going in the taxi to pick up the schoolchildren he could see Gerald going down Dibble Bank and Gerald would see him and would turn round as though he was coming up and wave for a lift. Derrick had to pretend he didn't see him waving. He did pick him up sometimes, but not when he was doing the school run. Derrick thinks he once had a sister, and that when they were children their mother went away on holiday with her and never came back. Linda thinks that eventually he "went into a home".

Getting a lift to school, Botton Hall and a little Jersey Cow

The way to school was remembered. Hilda said that she had two or three miles to walk and she and as many as maybe twenty children would climb onto the top of the milk cans and have a free ride to school. Bessie remembers getting a ride on the cans to Broadgate, and Emma remembers getting a ride on George Mortimer's milk wagon from Westerdale every Saturday, just riding on the back with the milk cans. They don't remember anyone ever falling off. Hilda remembers Harry Dowson piling children into his car, and often he would put the lads into a trailer he had behind to take the sheep to market. She said he was very good to them.

Annie Gaines

Annie said that when she was walking to school someone from the Botton Hall family used sometimes to come past in their car, but they would pick only the youngest children up and give them a lift so usually Annie had to walk! Annie worked at Botton Hall all her working life. She remembers Derrick coming up shooting, and she had to get him his dinner ready.

Derrick remembers going up to Botton Hall with a little Jersey cow. He bought the cow from Botton Hall, because he used to do all their taxi work. He "had the privilege" of taking the cow back there to the bull. "So when I took it to the bull I would slip Annie's Dad, who was the herdsman there, a couple of quid. It was quite a while after that I picked up the Botton Hall secretary, Mrs Gibson, in my taxi. She said, "I see you've had your cow up to the bull." I said, "How do you know?" She said she'd seen the entry in the book. Annie's Dad was so honest he'd paid the two pounds in, when really it was meant for him!" After that, instead of the two pounds, Derrick used to take him some cigarettes. It was a long walk for Derrick and the cow all the way up Danby Dale to Botton Hall from the Mill, but "the cow always got in calf".

At the "back end of 2005" the Botton Hall family's grandson called to see both Derrick and Annie. He told Derrick that Derrick's father had taught him to drive. Annie said she'd also met the family's Nanny in Norfolk, when she hadn't seen her for forty years. They've kept in touch with Christmas cards.

There was a big staff up at Botton Hall when Annie worked there, including a butler and a chauffeur. Derrick said that even though they had a chauffeur and a car, Derrick and his father used to do their taxi work, so perhaps they didn't use the chauffeur so much. One lady used to come out with half a dozen coats on, Derrick said, and rugs, but he used to turn the heater up and before they got far she was taking them off again.

More War-time memories

The discussion turned to memories of Danby Beacon. There was an early warning station there during the Second World War. It had eight "towers", or aerials. There were many British RAF people there, as well as American and Polish servicemen and women. There was quite a social life going on, and a picture house, which local people were invited to visit. Derrick didn't ever go to the picture house at Danby Beacon but Annie, Emma Skidmore and Hilda went, though they can't remember what the films were. They said it was all they could afford! Hilda remembers going to the picture house on her pushbike. Some local girls made friends too at Danby Beacon, and at least one couple got married. The servicemen came down to the villages to dances.

Evacuees came to the villages from Hull and mainly from Middlesbrough. There were quite a few at Danby School, Hilda said. She was only about ten years old at the time. Some of them stayed maybe only for a week, but others stayed for longer. The Miss Wards had three who stayed for a long time, one called Michelle and another Doreen. There were the Protherows with Mrs Mead, and Luke Scott had the Parkins in Castleton. None of them stayed to live here, but some have visited since. Emma said that a couple came to a coffee morning a few years ago. The man had stayed in Danby Dale, but he couldn't remember which farm he had stayed on because he wasn't very old at the time. Hilda said that the Swales family took in their nephew as an evacuee from Hartlepool.

Derrick in RAF Uniform

Derrick brought memories of Danby Beacon up to date. A couple who met there at Danby Beacon during the war were then married. They have come back to Whitby or to this area for their holidays every year since they were married. Now the lady has died, and her husband came to see Derrick a fortnight or so ago. He was looking for a tool that would dig a hole to bury two urns of ashes together locally, his and his wife's. Derrick told him he's looking ahead a bit, because the man is still alive! It just so happens that Derrick does have a special tool that would do the job. It used to belong to Mr McKinnis, but he's gone now.

Derrick met Enid, an usherette at the cinema where he took taxi customers, and they married in 1939. He said he was the first to go to the War from around here. He, Tom Armstrong and Doug Booth were all the same age, within a few months of one another. Doug could stay at home because he was farming, which was a "reserved occupation". Tom, a butcher's lad, wanted to be in the police force. He used to come every morning and ask Derrick, "Have you got your papers yet?" He was worried that the "Call Up" papers would come through before he got the police job. But they didn't and he did get into the Police Force. Tom joined at Whitby and did well. Hilda said he got to be a detective eventually, working in Northallerton. He used to go to race meetings. He married a lass from Leyburn way.

Derrick's wife Enid

Rosehips & Gardening

Frank Fishpool

Frank Fishpool told how during the war, and for quite a long time after, the teachers used to take out one class of children at a time to pick rosehips. The children could go out of school time picking in the evening, but they had to avoid the places where the school picked. The teachers sent the rosehips away "to the Government", and they would be paid for them. The hips were made into rosehip syrup. Syrup was then sent back to the school, and the teacher would dose each child every day with a spoonful. "If you picked them in the evening, you could take your bagful and get threepence a pound for them. But if you picked them with the school in lesson times then the money went towards school funds." Linda said they were still doing that when she started school in the mid-50s. Bessie said that they used to pick along Westerdale Lane.

Frank Farrow said after the war the schools had their own plots of land to grow vegetables for school dinners. Each child had his own plot. There were about 10 plots in his school gardens and his was number nine. Frank Fishpool said the school at Castleton did the same. They used to go down to Didderhow to do the gardening. They used to walk across Hills Lane and across the fields to Didderhow and each class had its own spot. "Old Charlie Hay used to whip you round and see that everything was right. Nora Booth was the Cook at the school during and at the end of the war, and after we picked the vegetables she cooked them for school dinners."

Collecting for the bonfire. Clive and Peter Thompson, John and James Mercer, Bob and Frank Fishpool. 1945

Before the war, the children used to bring their own dinners, usually sandwiches. Frank Farrow said that even before that the schoolchildren grew vegetables so that they would learn how to garden. "There was a plum tree and an apple tree and children had to learn what diseases the trees got, and they used to put a sticky band around a tree if it had a certain thing wrong with it." Plots were numbered, and the children had to know how to look after them. Bessie said she thought the vegetables might once have been given to the poor folk and Frank said the vegetables that they grew were part of the war effort. Emma Skidmore said that the Westerdale schoolchildren grew their vegetables on Bagdale down at the bottom of School Hill and up on the other side. At Castleton, it was only boys who grew vegetables, but in Westerdale, the girls did too. Frank said at his school the girls used to do knitting and sewing while the boys did the gardening. Bessie said the girls' first sewing lesson was to learn to darn and to make a book mark.

Hams & Wagons

Frank Farrow told a story about a man called George Robinson. He used to sell hams on the black market in Middlesbrough during the war. He took one down to the station and got on the steam train to Middlesbrough. He put the ham on the luggage rack. "Then who should get in the carriage, but 'Bobby' Thompson. The policeman didn't say anything. Then when they got to Middlesbrough. George sat there, and the policeman said, "Well are you going to get out?" George said, "Aye, I'll get off in a minute." So Mr Thompson got off and went on his way and then George got out and took his ham off into town and sold it. He thought no more about it but about a month later he was driving from Castleton to Danby and saw Mr Thompson walking the along the road. So he stopped and said, "Do you want a ride Mr Thompson?" He said yes, he would have a ride, so he got in and they were driving along without a word being said. Then all of a sudden Mr Thomson said, "By, that was a grand ham you had on the rack that day, George!" He didn't miss a thing, did Mr Thompson."

The discussion turned to village policemen, and how people respected and trusted them. They took a pride in their beat, and they knew everyone. If the lads did anything wrong, said Linda, like her brother Phillip and Colin Cook, they would get a clip round the ear! That was PC Cooper who did that. Derrick said they used to wait in shop doorways and catch people misbehaving. You never knew where they were. People told them all that they knew. Folks stood on their doorsteps talking, and would tell the policemen a lot.

A man called George Robinson worked for North Eastern Railways, driving a wagon and delivering meal and parcels, etc. The driver after him was 'Squeaky Willie'. Squeaky Willie was often drunk. He tipped his wagon over a time or two, but he still came back to have another drink and they still employed him. He tipped it over, upside down at the top of Danby Bank. Somebody came along and said, "What did you do Willie?" He said, "I'm just draining it!" He worked for North Eastern Railways for many years, and was doing the job while the steam trains were running right up to the 50s and 60s.

An accident in Castleton

Being "in place", and Pathways

Bessie talked about getting work in her father's days, and in her youth. When you were employed on a farm it was called being "in place". You were hired. You worked for a whole year before you were paid, and you were paid once a year on November the twenty-third "all the money in one go". The first "place" that Bessie's father had was at Fife Hall at Skelton and he had a long wait for the seven pounds that he was paid. Emma's brother Bill once worked at the same farm on the same "place" that Bessie did. Bessie was working in the house because Mrs Sanderson had gone to into hospital and

Bessie had to look after the house and the two boys. Bessie and Bill had both gone out one night. Bessie said her brother Bill was "a Right Devil, to put it mildly". This particular night she was walking back with her boyfriend when Bill passed her. The last one in had to lock the door. Bill knew she hadn't come in, but he locked the door so that Bessie had to knock and wake the boss up. Bessie said "Bill thought I would get into trouble, but I didn't so that was one in the eye for him."

Derrick said that before the war the women used to walk all the way from the top of Fryup Dale to Danby Station with the baskets of butter that they had made, to put on the trains to be taken to Middlesbrough to be sold. The women bringing the butter to Danby Station would cut from Danby Castle to Easton Lane. Everybody walked

Danby Dale

wherever they needed to go, making and keeping to their own pathways. Bessie and her boyfriend would have been using one of these paths. All the mails and everything that came to the station were led out on horses and carts. Derrick said that that's why a lot of the tracks that are around the area were not proper paths. A lot of the paths were communal. People would take a short way home, maybe over a field.

"When the farm men on a night had nothing to do they stayed with their horses and sat in the buildings talking with their friends. That's what they did. So paths were made when people strolled along to visit other farms, taking shortcuts to get there. They were not actually public paths, just community routes made by people taking shortcuts." Bessie said "We would just go navigating, and cutting across the fields. There was a route from Castleton to the vicarage where we just cut across over the gate and made a

Westerdale

beeline over the fields. We didn't even bother with the bridleway. Nobody bothered. In those days, everybody walked everywhere. All the people were locals, but now there are lots of strangers." Frank Fishpool's Dad lived up at "Pyethorn" in Westerdale, right up at Esklets. "When he was a little lad he used to carry butter and walk to Ormesby market. He would take a direct route across country, but it was still a very long way." Derrick said that old Harry Cook, who lived on Westerdale Side used to walk to Thirsk races. He used to stop on the way, but he was still walking all that distance when he was in his 70s. Again, he took a direct route straight across the moors. He used to walk to Osmotherly to see his wife when they were courting so perhaps Osmotherly was where he stopped overnight on his way to Thirsk races and back. (Bessie recalled Mrs Cook passing her driving test in Stockton. Bessie and her husband Reg went with her to Stockton to the driving test centre. She was driving down the High Street and she drove straight towards a policeman who was on point duty. Reg said "Stop! Stop!" and she said, "I'm stopping!" She was "getting on", and they didn't really think she was fit to be driving. They told each other, "She'll never pass," but she did. Bessie remembers exactly when this was. It was in August 1949.)

Derrick said that during the 1914 -18 war all the army men who lived here in the Upper Esk Valley and came home on leave got back to York on the train, and then had no other choice but to walk. There was a pub open then at Hamer. There are just a few stones left there now. They used to stay there overnight and at other different places. They couldn't walk from York within the day because it was too far. One such soldier was Frank Raw. There was no choice but to walk in those days. That is how the paths were made.

All the miners used to walk from Castleton to Rosedale, making tracks along the shortcuts. There would be tracks from Shaw End up from Ugthorpe to Rosedale. The miners would set off from Ugthorpe at two or three o'clock in the morning to walk up to Rosedale to start work at six o'clock. They would stay there, do a week's work and then come back. They would probably set off after a shift finished on a Friday night and then walk back and get home late. They would have Saturday and a bit of Sunday off, just time to go to chapel or church. Then they would have to walk back again. Or maybe they would

George Mercer from Westerdale, a soldier in World War 1

go to the pub, suggested Derrick. The pubs closed at 10 o'clock, so then they would have to walk all the way back to Rosedale. "Perhaps that's why the tracks are a bit winding. They couldn't walk straight!"

Elsie suggested perhaps some of the older women in the valley are pretty tall because they had to do a lot of walking. Elsie is a prime example, because she walked miles. Bessie said people then didn't have allergies. They had proper food in those days. Frank said the animals they ate were fed on grass and natural things.

More about Hirings and Work

Elsie Mould told about the "hirings" that her Dad went to in Guisborough. "He used to go to Guisborough on the 23rd November, on Martinmas day. People who wanted a new lad or man to work went, and they were all there waiting to be picked."

"Or a girl ", said Bessie. Elsie said, "They came and lived with you and you kept them, did their washing and everything."

Hannah Dale (Raw), Lucy Raw (Dowey), Elsie Dowey (Mould), Mrs Dale. Elsie Mould's Grandmother, Mother, herself & her Great Grandmother

No one could remember hirings at Castleton even though there was a market there at one time. Bessie said, "Dad went to Ruswarp when he was first hired to live with a family in Skelton as an under horseman. He was hired for the year but the second year he didn't stay on at Skelton, he went to Goathland. He would be fourteen, just leaving school. I left school at thirteen!"

Frank said, "People left school at thirteen, and took a job. They went to work for a year. If they decided to stay or if the farmer wanted to keep them on they would stay "in place", or they could go back to the hirings and get hired by someone else. They had now left home and they usually got home only about twice a year. They only got paid once a year, but if they wanted anything during the year they could borrow off their "hiring". They would be given a sub, to buy a pair of boots or anything like that and then at the end of the year it was knocked off the wages that they were hired for."

Bessie said, "You had to provide your own clothes. Men wore corduroy trousers and boots with gaiters. A lot wore clogs. They were warm and hard wearing. I can remember my Dad putting straw in the bottom of our clogs because it kept you warm and it stopped them getting damp, the straw kept you dry. The clogs had wooden soles and leather uppers, they were clumsy but they kept your feet warm". Elsie said, "When you walked through the snow the snow clods made you taller and taller. We bought the clogs from the cobbler." Frank remembers getting his from Arthur Burke whose hut, before it burnt down, was near Castleton School. Then he moved to a shop in Ainthorpe opposite Congrave farm. Hilda remembers Mr Carter, a cobbler who made clogs at Ainthorpe. Mr Husband repaired clogs and shoes round the back of Medds behind Castleton High Street. Frank said, "Clogs were lethal things really. In winter there was no grip on them at all!" Hilda said "They were nasty if you got a kick from them!" Bessie had some boots, and Elsie remembers having high boots laced up to her knees.

Frank said, "Farm workers used to wear old sacks tied round their middles to keep their clothes from damage or even round their legs just to try and keep themselves warm and clean. Some of the workers had to sleep out in the buildings. It depended on who they worked for. Some of the farmers didn't even pay. They didn't really want workers but they had to have someone to help them out. They used to treat them just like dogs so the workers didn't stay the next year. But once they were contracted for a year that was it - they had to stop. There were some people who were hired and they stayed with the same family up till they died."

Elsie said, "Jack Booth stayed with the Mortimer's at Dale view and never moved anywhere else". If the workers got married there wouldn't always be room for them so they would find accommodation in the village. "Unless they married the farmer's daughter!" said Bessie. Emma's uncle stayed working at the same farm for fifty years and never married. Frank said, "Well they never got off the farms to meet anybody, when you think about it. In them days it wasn't a nine till five job, it was up at five o'clock in the morning and you would probably be working till midnight. The stable men had all the horses to do. In harvest time they worked all hours if weather was right."

Bessie said "If you had two or three men hired and they had spare time they would just stay in the stable and play games on the stable bin lids – a Merrill board on top of the corn bins. They didn't have central heating then and it was warm in the stable from the animals. They got their meals, and if it was a 'good meat place' they would stay. If it was a poor meat place, and some farmers were very poor, they didn't stay."

Hilda remembers threshing day. "We fed fifteen to eighteen men their ten o'clocks, their dinner and tea." Bessie said, "If it was a good meat place the farmer always got plenty of help, but if it was a bad place he didn't get anybody." A lot of women had to help with the work, to milk cows and feed calves, and they did as much work as the men.

Harvesting and 'stooking', thought to be in Danby Dale - a very old photograph

Hilda said, "They had to do the work in the house and look after the men too." Bessie said, "Some farmers' wives could bake scones a lot better than others. Some scones were 'sad' but they used to fill you up." Cottages were often tied to the job and Emma Skidmore remembers her dad was put out of his home twice. Frank said, "You had to touch your cap if you passed the gentry. There were a lot of people like that when I was a youngster. There was old Tommy Boyes, he was a real old type of gentleman and I can remember riding past on me bike one day and he always carried a whip in his hand. I rode past one day and I just said, "How do!" and he hit me with his stick and said, "I'm Mr Boyes!" Every time after that when I went past I used to say "good morning Mr Boyes!" and touch my forehead. You know he was that type.   Mr Boyes supplied horses for the army in the 1st world war. The thing was that a lot of these people had been officers in the army and had been used to it. That was what they expected when they came out; you were just subordinates." Bessie said, "You always spoke to people as Mister or Missus, and as children we had loads of Aunties and Uncles who were no relation whatever." Hilda remembers her brother working for the family at Botton Hall. He used to wear a chauffeur's uniform and had to touch his cap every time he saw them.

Remembrance Sunday after the First World War. The family from Botton Hall is in the horse and cart.

Sunday Best - Traditions

Every one remembers having 'Sunday best' clothes. Emma said, "However poor you were you still had your Sunday best. We always had a dress and a little bonnet, and we got a new Easter bonnet. Frank said, "There was a room in a house where you couldn't go unless you were dressed up. Some house weren't very big but they had a parlour. Grandma lived in Moorsholm in a biggish house and we used to go there and all stayed in one room, but if you went on a Sunday and you were dressed up you were allowed in the parlour. It was all set out beautiful, and there was a piano in there." Hilda agreed, "It was for Sundays, or if the Vicar came to call. You hadn't to go in Grandma's Parlour, you just peeped in, you daren't go into it. I remember an organ. On Sunday we weren't allowed to do any work. We weren't even allowed to knit. On Sundays the farm workers weren't allowed to put the horses to work, you could just do things by hand. Good Friday was always a day for working in the garden. You always plant your tatties on Good Friday."

Bessie said "We could read, but generally only the bible. We used to walk to chapel from Woodend down to Westerdale. Good Friday was the day you horn-burned the sheep, to put the farmer's mark on the horns so you could tell who they belonged to. It wasn't a day of rest but you couldn't do your usual work. But jobs like that and gardening was what you were allowed to do. The war changed everything, because after the war everything went completely different. We hadn't known anything else, but all those traditions started to go after that."

Betty Taylor's Great Grandma Grainger lived at the "Diving Duck" Inn, Commondale

Frank said, "You could go for a walk every Sunday, usually after dinner. We would walk up to Danby church and down by Westerdale, across the fields, then about once a fortnight we would walk to Moorsholm, up by Dimmerdale to my Granny's." Hilda said "We used to walk through Park Woods". Emma remembers walking through Mill Wood. Frank remembers a proper path along the mill stream.

Poultry & Pigs

Bessie recalls, "Towards Christmas there were goose killing days, when you killed your poultry for Christmas. We always did it on the 18th of December, duck, geese and turkeys."

Hilda said, "One year Bessie's Mother was in hospital and we had over a hundred birds to dress and we had little children to look after, and they lost their dummies in amongst the feathers. That was the year that Bessie decided that she was NEVER doing that again. Elsie Dowson called to see us and one of the children was scratching.... "Hast thou got a dickie trodger?" she said. Those are the mites found on poultry."

"Elsie came to do the meals because Mother was in hospital." Bessie said. "Elsie also helped with the ploating. What a day that was. My arm was all swollen from pulling the leaders, drawing the feathers, it used to be hard work. There was only really the two of us (Hilda and Bessie). Dad helped a bit and Herbert would be killing them. You had to pluck them when they were warm. It was easier. The back room was full and we had trestle tables full of birds, then the next day we had them all to weigh and parcel up and deliver. I said then that was my last one. I had Robert and Leslie, and Hilda had Janet and was expecting. I can still see them looking for the dummies among the feathers.

And then you had all to clean up ready for Christmas. But that was one of your money making things, so you could buy Christmas presents. But by Christmas day you were jiggered. We didn't even get a day off to go to Middlesbrough to spend it that year."

Bessie said, "Everyone kept a pig and every kitchen had hooks in the ceiling to hang up the ham until it dried out, and then we had a bacon house". Frank said "We never had ours off the ceiling! It was hung up there and a piece was cut off when you needed it. George Williamson had a shed at the back of the Robin Hood with benches on. Everybody had a pig killing day and everyone had a separate place on these tables. You used to lay your pig out and cure it, then the following week someone else would kill their pig and lay it out next to yours and by the time you had got them all laid out the first ones were about ready".

Rick Champion with the family pig

People sometimes found it hard to face killing the family pig. When on a taxi run one day Derrick bought the pig pictured above as a tiny black 'reckling' piglet. He brought it home in his car boot. When he lifted the boot lid it was sitting in the spare tyre looking up at him. It was a great character that the family grew very fond of, and it lived a long life. It had ten litters of ten - that is one hundred piglets in its lifetime!

Hilda said that the Mell Supper is really more about the pig killing than about the harvest. "You always killed a pig with a mell. The mell was a hammer that was used to hit a bolt into the pig's head." Frank said, "It was a celebration for all the people who had killed a pig and to share the food. Pig killing started in September and went on until December or January. Every other house in the village had a pig and when you killed your pig you would go round and share the offal with every one. You couldn't eat it all yourself because there was too much. Then they would do the same for you. The bacon and ham was kept and cured". Frank said, "It was a real good do, pig killing day. At night the men would play nap (cards) for pennies." Bessie said, "Next morning you went to see who could find most pennies under the table that the men had dropped 'cos we'd had to go to bed. They had their home brew, gale beer, Mother used to make a lot of gale beer. Do you know there is still gale growing at Lieth House!" (Gale is bog myrtle.)

"One household would do the pig killing one week, and someone else another time," said Bessie. "There was a piece of meat and apple pie because there were a lot of apples at that time of year. The ears and the trotters were used to make brawn. My mother used to put shin beef with it to make it go further." Elsie said, "An old hen would often do." "The one that had died," said Frank. "Nobody knew any different, it made it spread out!!" Bessie said, "Well you had to put something with the trotters but they made good jelly!!" Frank said, "Sometimes the pig would get up and run! I can remember them chasing one round the Robin Hood yard until it dropped. The blood from a pig was collected and made into black pudding and shared with your neighbours. The pig was put into a big wooden tub of boiling water and then scraped clean You made black pudding, and the fat was rendered down to make lard for the winter. We used to blow the bladder up to play football."

Cars, mills & electricity

The first cars were in this area in the early 1920s. There were not many, and there were none parked up by the roadside in the villages as today. Fred Flintoff had an old Alvis, and Uncle John Featherstone in Westerdale had a car and he had a garage that was "straight through" so that he could drive it into one end and out of the other. "He couldn't reverse it, so when he went shopping in Castleton he drove the car down the hill towards the station and round and back to Westerdale so that he didn't have to turn round." Miss Mortimer had a car and the Bonases had one, which Emma Skidmore said they had when she was a little lass, and she was born in 1932. Norman Standford bought Uncle John's old Jowett. Sid Beeforth and George Mortimer had cars, and John Scarth who had the shop in Castleton had a milk wagon. Bessie said some of these vehicles are buried in the old dam at Broadgate. When they moved in there in 1946 Bessie's dad wouldn't let them go where the mill race and dam was until it was filled in because the water was very deep, and they put the old cars at the bottom when they filled it. Derrick said they will have rusted away by now. The dam and mill race were there to drive the mill wheel and the farmer had ground his own corn at Broadgate, but the mill wasn't working when Bessie's family moved in. There was another mill in Westerdale beyond the cricket field.   Frank said that there were a lot of mills in those days. There were two in Castleton with one by the Esk and one at Ashfield's. There was one at Danby. There was an old mill race coming down through Mill Woods.

Dale End , Danby village. There is a turf stack ready for use by the blacksmiths , Lesley & Eric Snaith who worked with their father, by then an elderly gentleman. There are implements waiting to be repaired. The low building beyond the bus is Eric Huntroyd's garage, with petrol pumps.

Frank said that in those days in Danby there were two lorries that belonged to Montrose, the electricity people. The electricity was generated by the mill wheel in Danby. He said it gave not a bad light, and he doesn't remember candles much. Derrick remembers moving into the corner house at the bottom of the High Street in Castleton in about 1940, and they still had oil lamps then. The Punches wouldn't put electricity in at first because it was going to cost them too much, so it must have been 1946 or '47 before they had electricity. And then it was just one light. Elsie said they didn't have electricity at Howe Wath for a long time, and they had to carry water from over the road. Linda said that when her family moved to Westerdale in 1952 there was no electricity there. Bessie said her family had a generator.   Frank said that in Danby Eric Huntroyd produced electricity at his garage behind the shop which was down the road on the opposite side to the Duke of Wellington. No one could remember how it would have been paid for. Perhaps people paid for it when they went in for their papers. Eric produced his own, but then was bought out by the Electricity Board.

Riverside Drama at Castleton

In February 2007 present with the group at Danby Teashop was Miss Marion MacDonald, the daughter of Mr Niel MacDonald who was the vet in Castleton for forty years, from the early 1930s to the early 1970s. She remembered a story from her childhood.

Marion remembered : "It was Sunday morning and we had all gone for a walk. Dad was working so he wasn't about. We went down to the bottom of the hill and I can remember quite clearly hearing Ian saying, "Mummy! Kirsty's in the river!" and Mum saying, ""Well tell her to get out!" Well, of course, she didn't.   She couldn't get out because I think she had probably stood on a piece of the bank side that had given way under the snow. It was just when the snow of 1947 was melting.   It was March, and Kirsty had just been four.   The next thing I can remember seeing was this child floating off under the bridge on the top of the water and my

Mr. N. MacDonald, Castleton veterinary surgeon & his family.
Kirsty , Isabel, Marion, their father Niel, Ian, their mother Freda and Barbara.

mother hurtling down the bank. Do you remember the old rabbit skin gloves with the big gauntlet tops? I can quite clearly see her throwing those off onto the bank side and saying to me, "Look after Isabel," because she was less than two – about nineteen or twenty months – and Ian running like the clappers over the bridge to find help.

Fortunately Alwyn Champion and Ray Husband were working at their garage which was down by the "Eskdale", or Station Hotel. They came with ropes and various things. How on earth they all ever survived I just do not know, because when I think back to it now, the river was almost up to the bridge arch. It was really full, and really flowing hard. Mum got Kirsty and grabbed hold of the branch of a tree, and managed to keep hold of it long enough for Ray to come and get Kirsty from her and get her out. Then she lost it and went on further down the river.   Alwyn eventually got her out too.

71

We were living at "Hill Crest", and I can remember Dr Armstrong coming, but neither of them even got a bad cold. It was just incredible really. We were all dressed up in winter clothes, with top boots or wellingtons and things and they helped Kirsty to float, really. I can still see her on the top of the water drifting off, and not looking at all worried about it. She was always in trouble! The water was so cold – floating ice and so on.

My mother was a very good swimmer. She'd lived at Saltburn as a girl and she'd swum in the sea every morning before she went to work. It was a good job, because most people wouldn't have survived the cold, apart from everything else. I haven't really thought about it for years, but then Kirsty sent me the cuttings from the newspaper at the time about it, and it brings it all back to mind again. Kirsty doesn't remember it. She was only just four. But I'm sure everybody here remembers it." Everyone agreed that they did remember it.

A newspaper article from the time. It differs little from Marion's memories but the phrasing is so different from newspaper reports today.

March 1947 Whitby Gazette

"MOTHER'S GALLANT RESCUE
Riverside Drama at Castleton.
Child Slipped Into Water.

There was a dramatic river-side rescue at Castleton on Sunday, at a time when the River Esk was in spate, and when considerable stretches of the river were in flood. Mrs. N. MacDonald, wife of a Castleton veterinary surgeon, was taking her four children aged seven, five, four and two, for a walk by the river, and Kirsty, the four-year-old daughter, slipped and fell into the Esk. The incident occurred near the bridge, and, carried by the current, the little girl disappeared under the bridge. Mrs. MacDonald immediately ran across the roadway of the bridge, and jumped into the water, catching hold of Kirsty who was being carried downstream by the swiftly flowing waters. A strong swimmer, Mrs. MacDonald, supporting the little girl, made for the side of the river, and grasped a bush. She was unable to regain the bankside because of the current and she clung on in the hope of assistance being forthcoming.

The three young children by the side of the river shouted for help, and Mr. Alwyn Champion, working in his nearby garage, and Mr. Raymond Husband, his assistant, rushed to the spot to be told by the children "Mother is in the beck." Mr. Husband immediately entered the water. He could swim, and while he made his way to where Mrs. MacDonald and Kirsty were in the water, Mr. Champion, a non-swimmer, returned to his garage for a rope. Mr. Husband seized the child from the mother who, by this time, was almost exhausted. She was unable to retain the grasp of the bush, and while Husband grasped the bush and held the child, Mrs. MacDonald was swept away downstream. Mr. Champion, returning with the rope, saw what was happening, and running along the bank side, he threw the rope to Mrs. MacDonald, who seized it and was dragged through the water to the bank.

Messrs Raymond Husband & Alwyn Champion, "who played a noteable part in the rescue of Mrs N. Macdonald and her daughter Kirsty on Sunday morning"

72

She refused to leave the river, however, insisting on returning to the place where Mr Husband and her child were in the water. When she and Mr. Champion got back to the bridge they saw Husband was having difficulty to retain his hold on the bush for the intensely cold water had caused him to have an attack of cramp. He was holding the little girl's head above the water, but was powerless to move. Realising that assistance must be given to his workmate, Champion tied the rope to a tree, and grasping this he entered the water, and with the rope to support him he made his way across the stream and reached Husband, giving him assistance, and relieving him of the child.

By this time a considerable crowd had gathered at the scene, and onlookers brought a number of planks which they threw across the beck to make an improvised bridge. By this means they were able to bring Kirsty and her rescuers to safety. Mrs. MacDonald and Kirsty were taken to the Station Hotel, where they were attended by the local doctor. The little girl suffered no ill-effects from her experience, but Mrs. MacDonald was confined to bed with shock. There is no doubt but for her pluck and presence of mind her daughter would have been drowned, and Messrs. Champion and Husband also acted with commendable promptitude and courage. The river was in spate, following the thaw, and instead of being the usual placid stream, was a rushing torrent of water.

This is the second occasion upon which Mr. Champion has effected a rescue from the river at Castleton. The former incident which occurred before the outbreak of war in 1939 also concerned a four-year-old child who had slipped into the water, and, on that occasion, Mr. Champion's gallantry earned for him a commendation from the Police.

Neither he nor Mr. Husband were any worse for the part they played in Sunday's rescue, Mr. Husband quickly recovering from the attack of cramp, and both were at work on Monday."

The Esk River running through the valley at Castleton, the bridge to the lower right. A quiet day in this photograph, the Mill in the foreground, the station beyond, and the old Ganister Mill at the middle right edge of the picture.

Emigrating to Canada

In 2007 Jane Wiggins from Canada wrote :

John & Isabelle

"John Breckon, a farmer's servant from Westerdale, and his wife Isabelle came to Canada in 1831 with "the desire to better their circumstances" - John was born 1803 in Westerdale, one of 5 children. John and Isabelle along with his brother Joseph and his wife Maria Cooper Breckon sailed from Whitby to Canada in 1831. Joseph and Maria were killed on a steamer when the boiler exploded when going through the Lachine rapids in the St Lawrence River. John and Isabelle settled in Nelson County of Halton with about 12 pound ten - they purchased 152 acres of farmland on credit for one pound per acre - in 1853 this land was now valued at 2300 pounds. There have now been 6 generations of John Breckons in Canada - the youngest is now in his late 20s."

Frank Fishpool's Grandfather Harry was born at Pyethorn near the Esklets at the top of Westerdale and around the 1890s he went to Canada. There were a lot of people at that time who did the same. Derrick remembered, "Some Chipchases went from Rosedale to emigrate and my mother had a photo of them all on the ship's railings", and Bessie said, " The Robinsons went from Winsley Hill in 1900 something."

Many came back to this area eventually. Hilda said her Grandfather came back. He was born at Westerdale. Soon afterwards his family had sailed to Canada and two of his brothers were born there, but they came back - she thinks it was because it was so cold over there! Derrick said, "My Grandad had an uncle who took his family over there. The whole family got something wrong with them and they died, and he had to bury them all himself in the garden. As years went on they were dug up again and given a decent burial. The uncle said to my Grandad that when he was in a position for him to go over he would send for him. When Grandad was an old man his uncle sent word to say that he *was* in a position were he could receive him, but he advised him not to go."

Frank said that when people got to Canada they were given a piece of land. "It didn't take them long to buy a bit more. If they bought two acres they got another two to go with it so they had four acres." Hilda said that the Robinsons from Winsley Hill had a great big farm. She had visited them and it seemed to be miles to walk around a field. Bessie agreed. "They stayed there and they did well. When they where cutting corn they would have maybe a dozen combines."

Derrick said, " Well at one time if you fenced a bit if land in this area you could claim it. If you go over the top to Hob Hole you can see lines in the land where they were going to put up walls. They didn't get it done before their permits ran out, so they didn't get it claimed. That's how all the little garths were built."

T Watson WLPS

Hob Hole, 1910

A Letter from Canada written by Allin Swales who left Applegarth Farm, Fryup (with his brother? Frank), to Mr Frank Raw of Ajalon House, the Farm Adjoining.

c/o Mrs Toop
Nutana P.O. Sask.
Canada, June 3rd 1913

Dear Friend,

We arrived out safely to Canada. We had a fairly good voyage. We were detained a day or two in the fog just off Newfoundland, thus making us eight days instead of six upon the water. We landed in Quebec on the Saturday morning. After waiting about for about half a day we at length found our train and after buying some provisions we started off from Quebec at 2.30 o'clock. We had two days and two nights betwixt Quebec and Winnipeg. We arrived at Winnipeg at about 10 on Monday night. We saw nothing of the town as it was dark. At 25 minutes to eleven pm after changing trains we left Winnipeg for Saskatoon. At about 9 in the morning we had a car off the rails which detained us for an hour. We arrived in Saskatoon at 15 minutes past five and went off and put up for the night. The next day we sought out Will Newton and stayed with him for three days after which we got a job or more correctly we stayed with him for five days altogether.

We started work on the 19th day of May at 19 dollars (£6.5s.0d) per month. We are busy in a little garden of 160 acres. We are going to have 35 acres of onions and carrots, lettuce and such stuff, 50 acres of potatoes and I fancy the other lot will be filled with turnips and cabbages and I don't know what else. We have been busy planting potatoes for more than a week and have not quite finished as we have another half day yet. We have a machine for planting potatoes one row at a time. Boss says he will have a machine to plant three rows at a time next year. He intends taking 600 acres next year and starting mixed farming. He only came out from England on the 17th day of April so we have got no buildings much. He says we are to stay with him for the winter too as he will have plenty of work for half a dozen men through the winter. Also he is going to have about 100 pigs so I think I will put in for pig feeder. We have hit upon a fair good meat house though it is different to English fare. Jack Payne is the name of the man who has the house. We are about 3 or 4 miles out of Nutana. There is a new tram line in operation from Nutana to Sutherland. Sutherland is our nearest railway station and next station to Saskatoon. Also there is to be a 5 day exhibition in Saskatoon in July. The tram line is to be finished for the occasion. Frank and I will have a day off when that day comes.

It's a beautiful country, very level and the air is very clear making it that you can see for miles. Distance deceives you too. If you think it is about a mile from where you are to another place further off and start to walk it, it will turn out nearer two. We are quite settled here too. Mr Toop says if we have any companions who would like to come out he will fit them up all right. I think that is all this time. Hoping you keep in the best of fashions.

I am yours respectfully, Allin Swales.

Three beautiful photographs loaned by Annie Gains of young people having fun on Castleton Cricket field. She doesn't know who they are or when, but the Reminiscence group thinks the roller is the same one used today. Notice the bridge, the Eskdale Inn and the track line to the old Gannister Mill beyond.

More young people below, many decades later, enjoying themselves in very much the same way at a Young Farmers Rally.

Conversations in Cottages
in The Upper Esk Valley
on the North York Moors

As part of the Westerdale Millennium celebrations
I visited some of our older residents in their homes
to talk about and record some of their memories.
Then Chris and Peter Knapp did the same, visiting
friends in Danby and Ainthorpe.

An afternoon with Joyce Middleton in her house in Danby in 2005.

Joyce in 2005

Joyce is 89 years old, and was at Danby School probably from 1921 until 1933. There were about 90 pupils, and boys, girls and infants were separated in the playgrounds. There were no school dinners and children brought their lunch in. Boys took potatoes to put round the closed stove in the classroom (turning them at break time) with their initials carved in to show which was whose. Everyone walked to school, except for two who came on a pony and trap.

Behaviour was very good. Girls never got caned but boys did. In the lessons very much time was spent in developing good handwriting, practising exact strokes in books that were marked out like music scores. There were competitions to find the best handwriting. The children learned reading by the phonic method. Many poems had to be learned by heart, and pupils might be asked to stand up and recite one at any time. In maths, tables were learnt by heart.

The girls did lots of sewing. They were taught how to measure themselves, to draw out paper patterns on squared paper and to make garments such as nightdresses. They knitted pink wool vests with large needles. This was not popular - they hid if they could.

The boys grew vegetables.

Children could stay at school until they were 14 years old, but some of the brighter ones were able to go to Whitby School, and there they could stay and take School Certificate. Some children who would have been able enough to go were needed at home or on the farm, or their parents couldn't afford the train fare.

Joyce Middleton as Rosalind in 'As You Like It' (with Danby Church Players) in 1934. Her maiden name was Robinson.

A Village Anecdote, written by Joyce

You have to think back a long way, to the early 20th century, and the recent discovery of "the wireless", which was to change our lives - for the better one wonders?

Eric Huntroyd, who brought Electricity to Danby by harnessing the power of the Mill Dam and the water wheel down by the Mill, (incidentally, when the light jumped and flickered which it did quite frequently my Dad would say "There's a salmon in the wheel!") However, that's by the way -

Anyway there was going to be the first Royal Broadcast, given by King George V at the Empire Exhibition at Wembley, in 1924, so Eric decided he would demonstrate the marvel of wireless to anyone in the village who was interested. He (Eric) lived with his

mother in the house now occupied by Bill Beattie. He rigged up some kind of system on the front of the house - a big loudspeaker thing facing the Chapel Green. There would be some complicated wiring arrangement we couldn't see, of course. He put the word around that all were welcome to go and listen to this "magical" event. (A public broadcast was highly illegal at the time, but I don't think anyone was cast into prison.)

Danby Chapel

So a considerable number of folks gathered on the green in front of the Chapel - I don't recall the exact day, (it was the 23rd of April) but it was warm and sunny. I remember sitting on the little hilly bit, in front of where the Wilsons live now. (This was formerly a little grocery shop kept by the Misses Easton.) I was 7 years old.

When the broadcast began the King's voice reverberated round the green and the houses, and it sounded very TINNY. I can't remember what he said, but it would be the usual praise for the inventors of this modern miracle, and all the good it would do in the world.

Everybody seemed very impressed, and no doubt it encouraged people to buy a wireless set: and no doubt it would do Eric's business good, as all the batteries which were used to make the wireless work had to be taken to be re-charged at Eric's garage. Big, heavy cumbersome things were those accumulators!

Eastons Stores in Danby

Reminiscing with Bob and Daisy Cornforth in 2005.

Daisy & Bob Cornforth have been together for fifty-three years. They were married in the month of May. They'd known each other since Bob was ten years old and Daisy was nine, though Bob's mother had brought Bob and his brother, when they were around a year old, to call at the farm at Moorsholm to see Daisy's family not long after Daisy had been born. Bob and his brother were twins, and so were Daisy and her sister. Also Bob's aunt had married Daisy's uncle. It took Bob fifteen years after they left school to ask Daisy to marry him. Bob was thirty-one when they were married and Daisy thirty. They'd known each other all that time, living in the same area as each other, attending Young Farmers clubs and so on. Daisy said he took some catching! Daisy and Bob have fifteen grandchildren. One of their children has ten of his own, and another has four, including a set of twins, and another has one daughter.

DANBY.

Daisy & Bob really got to know each other when they went to Danby school. Bob came from Lealholm to Danby when he was nine years old, and the following year Daisy came from Moorsholm to Fryup when she was nine years old. At Danby school they were put in Mr Lyness's class, (Daisy had been moved up from standard four in Moorsholm) and Daisy said, "Every week, when Mr Lyness took your marks, he moved you. And when you got up to the top for ten weeks in the year you got an extra prize". They both have that prize, and Daisy got one each year for two or three years.

When Daisy was at Moorsholm school the children wrote on slates. They began writing in sand sprinkled on the slates, making "pot hooks", but then they graduated to a slate pencil and began to write. Slate pencils were horrible things. They squeaked! At seven years old, or nearly seven, depending on how bright you were, you were given a pen. It wasn't a biro - they didn't have those in those days even when Daisy and Bob left school - it was a pen with an inkwell and blotting paper.

Daisy's father, who was born at Danby, had gone to Danby School and Daisy still has one of his schoolbooks. When Daisy's family came from Moorsholm up to Fryup Daisy and her brother and sister wanted to go to Danby School. A friend of Daisy's who came from Lythe

The older children at Danby School in 1914, before Daisy's time.

to the Coombes to live with her grandmother wanted to go to Danby School too. She and Daisy had sat together when they were at Moorsholm School so when her family moved here the same year as Daisy's family they wanted to go to Danby together.

But there had been scarlet fever and also diphtheria in the valley and Danby School had been closed that year. So Daisy's Dad said they'd better go to Fryup School. The trouble was that it was further away from where they lived than Danby School. It was a long walk, and there were very few cars. They didn't like it at school there at all. The teacher had thirty odd pupils all of different ages, and she couldn't do justice to them all. Daisy and her sister and friend had just been moved up into standard 4 at Moorsholm, the week before they came (they moved them in April then) but the teacher at Fryup School said she couldn't do with any more children in standard 4. She didn't even try them out to see what work they had done! So they had to do the same work again that they'd already done, and the other school children there saw them as strangers, and they were not welcomed. Only a couple of years ago Daisy met the daughter of the next school mistress to be there at Fryup and she remembered that she too was a 'foreigner' for a long time. People didn't move much in those days, but stayed in one place, and were related to and all knew each other.

It was the same in a lot of places, but Daisy did not have that problem in Danby. The days at Danby School were the happiest in her life, Daisy says. She and her sister used to walk to school over the moor, carrying their lunch in a basket on a pole. Sometimes they walked on the road via Danby Castle - it was just a rough track, as tarmac didn't reach there till 1932.

Mr Lyness, the teacher at Danby School, was just, and very fair. If you tried to do your work he helped you. Bob agrees that they didn't know anyone who didn't like him. Other teachers at the school were Miss Collins and Miss Dunlop. The children called Mr Lyness "Loppy", but not to his face.

At Lealholm where Bob had been at school before he came to Danby School the head teacher was known for being "rough". Bob says he put him "over the desk" more than once. He did the same with a lot of the children. Daisy thinks that's why Bob's Dad moved the family when Gwenda, his sister who was five years younger, was starting school. There were four children in Bob's family, Bob and his twin, and Clarence and Gwenda. Daisy had her twin sister, and her brother, Howard. There was another boy in her family, born a year or two before the rest, but he only lived for a fortnight. Daisy and Bob were both children of farmers.

"Toadhole Cottage" - later removed for road widening - in Ainthorpe on the road up from Danby Bridge

Daisy's Dad was very particular, and very tidy. Theirs was the next farm to "The Jolly Sailors" near Moorsholm. Daisy's brother has a photo of the farm, and it's hard to believe how different it was then to now. "The chap that lives there now, who is a very nice man, just the same as everybody else, increased his herd and had a lot of stock. But now he's had to cut back and he's sold a lot of the land off. He works at a "leisure farm" at Thornaby now."

"Teapot Alley",Danby, in 1946, with the tap on the Green. This was higher up the hill from what is now the Bakery and is where there was a toilet with three holes!

Daisy's family had sheep, cattle, horses and pigs. They had a horseman and a younger lad. Her mother had no water in the house. There was a pump outside. There was no electricity. There were no tractors - there were horses to work, and they had to be taken to the pond to drink. They had to turn the cows out too to find water. There was no water trough. They started work very early every day, and Bob says they started young - "As soon as you could waddle, Daisy!" Bob's father's farm was up at Blackmire right up the dale, with cattle and sheep. Then the landlord sold it and the family went to Houlsyke to live. That's where Bob started school. Bob says they called Houlsyke "Sodom and Gomorrah, the City of the Dead"! There used to be a market at Houlsyke many, many years before Bob was there, and a bacon factory, which had just closed before they got there, where bacon was cured. Daisy says, "Gosh, when you come to think, things have altered that fast!"

Before the war many of the roads were not made up. Bob said 1926 was when the road by their present home was made up. Daisy said that when they lived by the "Jolly Sailors" there was a good tarmac road, and they used to visit her Granny, who lived at Castleton, in a pony and trap. Mostly Daisy's family walked, but for travelling long distances along that road they went in a trap, which was all right if it was fine but not if it wasn't! The roads were good to Danby and Castleton - they'd been tarmacked. But where the road came up Fryup - where the tennis court is now - the tarmac stopped. All the way around Frupdale it was just a hard flint road. The first summer Daisy was there, 1932, they came and tarmacked it. Daisy's father had the first tractor in Fryup. It had metal spade wheels, and she used to drive it.

Things changed when the war came. It was difficult to find feed for the animals. They fed barley to the pigs, but Daisy told her Dad that he'd be better selling the barley instead.

People came from Essex to escape the bombing and rented part of the farmhouse. Danby Beacon became a radar site with RAF and WAAF personnel, and there was even a "picture house" there, which locals could go to.

Daisy and her Dad used to collect the "night soil" once a week, and people used to sing -

> "My old man's a dustman
> And goes out day and night
> He wears a dustman's helmet -
> And comes home smelling of ...
> lavender and roses!"

Homeward bound

In 2005 Chris and Peter Knapp talked with Bill Beattie.

Bill is the only person telling a story in this book who was not born into, or married into a local family. His story is connected, though, because he is one of the cyclists often talked about who came from Middlesbrough to the villages for "teas", when out cycling in the countryside (mentioned in Emma's story, next). Bill knew how much his Dad liked this area and saw the house for sale. He called and a small boy said his father was in the pub. Bill found him there and made a deal over a fiver, then settled it later. He bought the house for his Dad, but he said his Dad was run over by a bus before Bill could tell him about it. He came in live in it himself in about 1965.

Bill, who is now in his 94th year, still does more than half an hour of exercises every morning and often walks 4 miles in a day. It's a habit he started when he got involved with cycling "road time trials", eventually becoming one of the most successful racing cyclists in the north of England. His first bike was made of parts taken from a scrap heap when he was fourteen years old. By sixteen he had a better one and was racing. In the late twenties and thirties bicycles had fixed wheels and no gears. Feet were fixed to the pedals with straps and clips and Bill says you did not get off your bike to climb up hills. He raced all over England, Scotland and in later years France and Spain.

Bill Beattie

He and his cycling friends would cycle all the way to the race venue to take part, be it Blackpool or Torquay. Because of lack of money they would overnight in farmers' barns - moving the cows over to find a warm spot. One night the only place six of them found to stay was in one double bedded room - they managed four on the bed crossways and two on the floor. They would be tired after all the cycling. They would stay overnight, race the next morning, and then ride back home again. Bill says that there's nobody who trains harder than racing cyclists if they want to be successful. All his club pals trained every day. After a day's work they would go home, have tea, then their bikes would come out and they would ride fifty miles. They raced every weekend. He raced from the age of fourteen for twenty years or more.

Bill also used to race on a wooden tracked velodrome at North Ormesby. Bill and his friends called it the "Board Track". It was like a "Wall Of Death", where you could easily slither into the middle - taking a lot of skin off! On Bill's right side he has a permanent scar from coming off the board track. It was at a forty-five degrees angle, and if you caught your pedal on the wood, down you would go, as many times he did.

During the war Bill worked as a boiler man, as an engineer and a plater. His was a reserved occupation. He and another lad from Thornaby were sent to the Clyde, to the Fairfield shipyard in Govern. It was an admiralty yard. He dealt with top-secret drawings and plans, working on repairing damaged ships. There were destroyers, battle ships, and aircraft carriers - all sorts of casualties of the war. Bill says sometimes the damage had to be seen to be believed. One was a cargo boat that had a hole right through it, from side to side, just above the watermark. It came in further down the Clyde. Bill wondered how it got back at all.

Reminiscing with Emma Beeforth of Westerdale in January 2001

Emma Beeforth was born Margaret Emma Knaggs, at Quarry Farm in Westerdale in 1920. She had a younger brother, William, and her father was a blacksmith working with his father in Castleton. After Emma was born they moved to Castleton for a while, but she lost her father when she was seven years old and her mother moved her family back to Quarry Farm, which was the home of her mother's parents. Grandfather Hartley was the agent for the estate, and he farmed milking cows, beasts, sheep, pigs and horses, and arable. He was born at Grange Farm in Westerdale, and

Emma with her grandparents when she was a very small girl

was one of eight children. Grandfather Hartley's brothers and sisters were William, Polly, Sally, Amelia, Beatrice (who was poisoned when she was housekeeping for someone), Charlie who went to New Zealand, Thomas who died when he was 14 falling off a load of hay, and then another boy born later, Tom Rawe Hartley who married a girl named Laura. Grandfather's family moved to Hall Farm, and then when he got married he moved to Quarry Farm, where his Aunt had lived. Her name was Hodgson and her grave is in Westerdale churchyard.

Westerdale Chapel Anniversary. Emma's Uncle David Hartley is the little boy with the basket, on the left.

Emma's mother, Beatrice Emma Hartley, was the youngest of seven children. The first of her mother's brothers and sisters only lived for a month. The next three, Mary Jane, David and Lucy, were born fairly closely together in age, but then Hannah Knaggs Hartley, Martin, and Emma's mother were born with five years between them. Emma's Grandmother and Muriel Mortimer's Grandmother were sisters. They were Knaggs, but were no relation to Emma's father. Grandma Knaggs was a Milburn. Grandfather Hartley's grown up children had all, except for Aunt Hannah, left their parents' home when Emma and her brother and mother moved back to Quarry Farm. Grandfather, who was getting older by then, was glad to have their help.

Emma's Aunt Hannah was a teacher at Westerdale School before the 1920s, walking there daily from Quarry Farm. Even in those days she earned £30 a year! She probably would have moved to work further afield, and she could have had a good position. But when her siblings left the farm to be married, she, as the "spinster of the family", was expected, and felt it was her duty, to give up her job and return to work on the farm. She was a workaholic, Emma says. She even used to scrub the farmyard once a week!

Emma went to school in Castleton until she was seven years old, and one afternoon when she was only five she got into trouble with Miss Meade because her knitting wasn't right. So, after that, on knitting afternoons Emma didn't go to school! She went home for her dinner, then without her mother knowing, she just didn't go back. When her mother spotted her playing in the street she took her back to school and talked to Mr Jackson, the head teacher, who said that he would make sure Emma was all right. And he did. After that Emma was at school in Westerdale until she was fourteen and a half, walking there each day from Quarry Farm in all weathers. There was a teacher there called Miss Dent in 1926, who took a ruler to Emma's knuckles! She did enjoy school generally

Castleton School in 1925. Emma is 4th child from left, front row. On the back row are: Sarah Dale, Tut Welford, Archie & Alex Findleson, Allan Miller, Ralph Williamson, Harry Thorpe, Susie Williamson, Mr Jackson. Front: Miss Tibbet, ?, Mary & Douglas Booth, Emma, Peggy Askew & brother, Ronnie Cook, Peter Jackson, Miles Cook.

though, and was quite sad to leave. There were two teachers, and about thirty children. That was fewer than there had been in the days when her aunts and uncles had been pupils.

Generally, Emma and her brother helped on the farm whenever they could. When Emma was about twelve she lost her front teeth while doing one of her regular chores. The young beasts had to be turned out at mid day to drink at the water trough. On this occasion she leaned across to reach the chain of one which had its head down, eating, when suddenly it flung up its head and caught Emma in the mouth.

She was taken on the train to the dentist in Middlesbrough. They had to walk to the station. No cars or buses then. They rarely went to either Middlesbrough or Whitby, because they couldn't afford to. Only for things like new shoes from Whitby or Middlesbrough. They had laced shoes, and were given no choice in style or colour. They had a pony and cart, in which they used to go to church on Sundays.

A highlight of the year for Emma when she was a child was Christmas. They'd wake up very early to see what was in their pillowcases. It was Grandad's birthday on Christmas Day as well, so they knew that all the cousins and aunts and uncles would be coming to visit. It was a

Emma in 1927, in the "Birds" fancy-dress her mother made

very busy day. Emma's Grandma, mother and aunt would have been cooking for days. Her cousins, Greta and Mary who lived in Westerdale village, would come to stay for about a week. The three girls were close in age, and Emma's brother William a little younger, and all great friends.

One Christmas the four children rehearsed the carol "Christians Awake" to perform for their relations. For the performance they went out of the front door and round to the back, singing lustily. Later they discovered they'd been heard to the end of the dale!

In the summer the two cousins would come to stay for a month's holiday. Emma remembers, amongst other games, building little huts out of bits of wood, and sacking to play house in, and "baking" mud pies, which they decorated with flowers.

Grandad and Grandma had their Golden Wedding in 1931, which was unusual and a big thing to celebrate. People didn't live so long in those days.

Emma & her brother in 1928, dressed for a party

Then Grandad died in 1933. Emma's Grandma died in 1936, so Uncle Dave and his wife Mary, who had been Mary Mercer, Jack, Charley, Bill, David and Mary's parents ~ (there was twenty years or more between Mary and her eldest brother) moved from the cottage in Westerdale, now known as "The Pastures", to Quarry Farm to take over the farm. Emma, her brother, mother and aunt Hannah needed to find somewhere to live. They moved to Ivy Holme in Westerdale, where Emma lives still, in April 1937. The previous owner was a Mr Esmarch, and his mother lived there before that. Previously, Ivy Holme had been the Post Office, run by the Miss Featherstones. They and Mrs Mortimer (Annie's mother) had the brick cottages opposite Emma (Rose Cottage) built, incorporating a new Post Office, and moved over there. Later the Post Office was moved again to Arkangel when Eleanor Hardisty, or Ellerby as she was then, took it on.

The Christmas after they'd moved to Ivy Holme, Emma's Aunt Hannah went to post a parcel at Westerdale Post Office in Rose Cottage and tripped over a sack which had been spread to protect the floor from snowy feet, and she broke a bone in the front of her knee. She was lame ever after. The doctor was called to her and he bound the knee up very tightly, promising to come back on a particular day. But he didn't come back. Around the bandage the knee began to turn black, so Emma's mother cut off the bandage with scissors.

Someone took Emma's aunty to the bone setter in Middlesbrough, who told her to apply heat and rub on some ointment that he gave her. That went on until September. Emma's Aunt Mary from Castleton and a friend of hers took Aunt Hannah to Dr English in Sleights. He told her that she could have an operation that would rid her of the pain, but that it would leave her with a stiff leg. And that bearing in mind her age (her forties) he advised her against having it done. She should use more ointment. It was awful. Aunt Hannah used to sit in a basket chair beside the fire. Emma would warn her that she was coming to put coal on the fire and she would say "Don't move your leg.." but sure as could be she always did, and it would be knocked, and Emma says she can still hear her aunt's shouts of pain. But they served teas in the cottage to passers by ~ cyclists and holiday makers, and Emma thinks it kept her aunt going, meeting all the different people who called.

Emma worked on her Grandfather's farm after she left school but when she moved to Ivy Holme, Emma's first job outside home was at "South View" in Ainthorpe, at Miss Lennard's boarding house. Emma was seventeen, and cycled there each day.

Then she worked at Hall Farm, for the Bonas family. The farm had sixteen cows, young beasts, pigs and horses. They also took in visitors sometimes ~ mostly holiday makers.

The farmyard at Hall Farm - but much later and very different, actually in 2006!

Threshing at Low House, Westerdale. Arthur Boyes, Jack Boot & Sandy Muir are on the machine, in front are Lesley Bonas Joe Sherwood, David Hartley, Rob Hood. The three at right end are Emma's brother William, her husband Sid, and John Muir.

When Emma began her job there were Mrs Bonas, Mr Bonas, Grandfather, two boys and two girls. The girls were Winsome, a five year old, and Dorothy who was two. Emma worked from 8am till 8pm. Sometimes Emma had to get Dorothy up out of her cot when she arrived in the morning and get her dressed. Two years later Mildred was born, and Emma grew very fond of her as she looked after her a lot. A day's work was begun by washing up the dishes. A major task was washing the clothes ~ lighting the copper, the clothes to boil, blue, get dry and iron. The washer had a hand agitator, and there was a hand wringer. The iron was heated in front of the fire, and had to be cleaned before it was used - such a hot job in the summer. Emma made dresses for the three little girls. Their washing and ironing alone, specially in the summer time was a considerable task.

The days of milk coolers arrived, and the cooler was put in the back kitchen adjacent to the cow bier, and cleaning the dairy floor which was green from boots trailing from the bier to the dairy was also a continuous job. The milk was taken in twelve gallon churns on the Bonas's milk float pulled by a horse to the station to be sent to be sold. Sometimes Emma helped with hay time ~ making haycocks, and at harvest to go and "pick on the stack" ~ catching the sheaves from the person tossing them up onto the stack, and passing them to the person stacking them. She occasionally milked if the others were busy in the fields. After a while they used an early electric milking machine not very different from the present ones. The paying visitors sometimes made life amusing. Emma used to have to "serve on". Listening to the conversation between a Wing Commander and his "wife", Emma and Mrs Bonas came to the conclusion that she perhaps was no such thing! Emma worked for the Bonas family till 1949.

Westerdale Home Guard
Back row: Willie Thompson, Jack Ellerby, Jim Mortimer, George Booth,
Middle row:Jack Booth, George Cornforth, Stan Featherstone, Fred Dowson, Bob Kerr,
Front: William Knaggs (Emma's brother), John Dowey

The War didn't make very much difference to life in Westerdale. Everyone had to be careful with the blackout. No one must show any lights. Then on light nights Emma used to watch our own planes going out overhead, and wonder if and hope that they would come back safely. People used to grow food to supplement rationing. Emma's family kept chickens and pigs. There was a search light at Arkangel and some soldiers were positioned there, and soldiers were camped at the bottom of the village. A young woman who was a hairdresser from London and her little girl stayed at the Bonas's farm during that time, to be near a corporal who was stationed in Westerdale. She went with him wherever she could. The soldiers were perhaps doing exercises here, and then in Helmsley, preparing for going off to France, Emma thinks. But they were the 22nd Dragoons, and they were the first into Dunkirk, and Emma often wonders whether the young woman's husband came home to her.

There was one shop in Westerdale run by Miss Shaw during the war, and before that as far back as Emma can remember it was run by Mrs Watson and perhaps her father before, in the cottage where Miss Ruff and Miss Longmuir now live. It sold groceries, paraffin etc. In the fifties Miss Shaw died and the house was bought by the Pages for a holiday cottage. They called it "The Craggen". Then Miss Ruff and Miss Longmuir bought it in 1966. The Post Office moved to Eleanor's care at Arkangel while she was Eleanor Ellerby, but when she married Bill Hardisty and moved next door but one to Emma she brought the Post Office with her to there. There hasn't been a pub in Westerdale in Emma's lifetime. Muriel Mortimer's uncle took the Duncomb Arms, but closed it. Emma always kept in contact with her mother's cousin, a nurse, who died aged ninety-seven in November 2000. The cousin used to visit Quarry Farm, once calling when Grandmother was quite ill. She also just happened to call as Uncle Martin died at the Downe Arms in Castleton, where he was landlord (which wasn't good for him) and she helped to lay him out. That was in the 1940s.

There was a blacksmith in Westerdale, a Mr Kemp, and Emma remembers a group of them going in to show Mrs Kemp how they were all dressed up in their costumes for a fancy dress ball, and Mrs Kemp was in bed. Emma's cousins, brothers Charley, Bill, and Jack Hartley, were a dance band for the dances, and the Jacksons from Broadgate Farm were another.

Uncle David Hartley was the organist at Westerdale church for many years, and when Emma's Grandfather was church organist, there was a choir of twenty-four people! Uncle David's daughter Mary Hartley was very musical, with a lovely singing voice and she was also the organist for many years at Westerdale church after her father, but was too little at that time to be in the dance band. One of the Jacksons married a Mortimer, Muriel's cousin. As Emma says, there were no motor cars and only cycling or walking, so people didn't get very far away to meet other people.

Emma in fancy dress (a beautiful old dress borrowed from Eliza Featherstone at Church Farm)

Dances, held in the Institute, were attended by people from all around the area ~ Commondale, Fryup, Castleton and Danby. They were held to celebrate events such as VE day, or for charity. The "Hospital Do" sometimes went on till 2am! There used to be some good dances, sometimes in fancy dress. They were held in Castleton too. They were for Christmas and Easter, Boxing Day and Harvest. Emma has a vision in her mind of the Harvest Dance, and one couple dancing in the Lancers. When the girl was swinging at the corners she always had her eyes closed! The dance goers walked to Castleton and back if a dance was held there, sometimes cold and wet in long dresses.

For Harvest Festival a service was held on the Friday. Emma remembers having to bring extra chairs into the church because so many people came. Miss Duncomb, and later it would be Lord Feversham, would arrange for a Harvest tea to be held at Westerdale Hall, to be served by the Parish Ladies. Everybody would be invited. All the children would be given a harvest gift, also donated by either Miss Duncomb or Lord Feversham. Emma still has a silk purse and a book that she was given. In later years the Harvest Tea was held in the Institute or the School Room (it still is).

Fifteen year old Emma in her first evening dress

In 1949 Emma left her job at the Bonas's farm and in 1950 she went to work "for so many days a week", for the Mortimers at Dale View till 1975. Emma also used to work, on Fridays, for Major Blakeborough (who could be quite "Hasty" at times).

Aunt Hannah died in 1960. Emma's brother William married Renee in April 1961, and Emma married Sid in October 1961. William and Renee were married in Danby Chapel. Emma and Sid had quite a big wedding ~ they were married in Castleton Church and the reception was at Danby Village Hall. Commander Howell and Major Blakeborough were there, and one or two doctors, and Emma and her mother did all the catering. Sid, Emma and her mother all lived together at Ivy Holme.

Sid was born in Sun Dial Cottage in Fryup, then he lived in Plum Tree Cottage in Danby. He used to work at Hall Farm and on other farms in his early days after leaving school. During the war he worked "on the War Ag", with tractors. After a while he was a foreman and he used to collect time sheets on Sundays. After the war he worked at Dibble Bridge, then he went to work for ICI, again with tractors to begin with, and then at a Water Treatment plant.

The serving of "Teas" at Ivy Holme went on till just after Emma was married to Sid. They had some regular visitors. A cyclist, Bernie Swanson, who had a cycle shop in Middlesbrough, came most Sundays for Sunday lunch, along with other cycling friends. Ivy Holme has often been full of visitors ~ that's why Emma has so many chairs in her cottage and more upstairs in case they're needed.

They bought their cottage as sitting tenants in 1966 for two hundred and six pounds and some shillings and pence. They bought it from the Mortimers. They added a back kitchen and a bathroom and small bedroom upstairs, and had to raise the ceiling upstairs to comply with building regulations. The remains of the post office grill and the post box in the wall outside can still be seen in her cottage. Emma's mother died in 1975, and Emma wanted to look after meals and so on for Sid who was on shift work by then, as her mother had been doing, so she gave up her job.

Social life was rather spoilt by Sid's shift work because he worked such odd hours. Sid used to make corn "stack" ornaments in his spare time ~ birds and different things, that were once said to keep away evil spirits. Sid had learnt how to make them in the sixties in a "five minute lesson" from Joe, an old friend on the War Ag. The first time Emma had a try she thought, "That's no good for me. I can get on with my knitting quicker!" But Emma was a member of the W.I. and they wrote to her asking her to make a corn dolly for the Danby Show WI Groups competition. It went on from there. Sid and Emma made more and more, and gave talks on corn dolly making and gave demonstrations. In 1969 Miss Hartley and Miss Ingleby, the local~history authors, came to Westerdale to see them, and wrote about their corn dolly making.

Emma in 2001 helping a Westerdale village group of neighbours with the art of "hooky rug" making

In Emma's youth her main way of getting about was walking, or riding her bicycle. Then the motor car arrived. Emma said, "In my life time I think there must have been more change than there'll ever be again when life back then, as it was in the closed world of Westerdale, is compared with life now."

Conversations in 2001 with Elsie and Arthur Dowson, who lived at Grange Farm, Westerdale, until 1999 when they moved to Castleton.

Arthur~

My family first came to live at Riddings in Westerdale in 1932, when Riddings was a little forty acre farm with about half a dozen cows, and a few beasts, a few sheep and a few hens . We grew an acre of potatoes, some turnips and a bit of corn. There were only two children in my family, me and my sister Heather.   I went to school in Westerdale.

***Westerdale School in 1934** – Teacher Grace Watson*
***Back row.** Left to right: Bill Hartley, Les Bonas, Stan Smith, Ian Hardisty, Tom
Mortimer, George Booth, **Arthur Dowson**, Ben Smith*
***Second row from back:** Earnest Bonas, Bessie Flintoft, Freda Taylor, Doris Lynas,
Mary Dale, Dorothy Taylor, Meg Booth, Eileen Dowey, Sandy Dowey*
***Third Row:** Bill Thompson, Tim Knaggs, **Front Row:** Herbert Flintoft, Joe Thompson,
George Taylor, Paul Hynson, Roll Dowey, Wilfred Flintoft, David Hartley*

While I was at school there would be twenty-eight or thirty children, and there was one teacher for a long time, and then there was a succession of them, one after another. There was a teacher called Miss Dent for a long time, who I don't remember. Miss Grace Watson was my first teacher, and Carol who brings the letters now is her granddaughter.

95

She left to go to Bainbridge after the School Governors ruled her out of her job of head teacher because she was going to be married to Mr Hardisty. In Church schools they wouldn't allow two incomes to come into one household. There was a Miss Adamson, Mrs Crabtree, Mrs Emmit and Miss Meggison, and a relief called Miss Fletcher, who Elsie had at Farndale.

When I was still at school we helped a bit in the hayfield in the summer holidays, and picked taties in potato picking week but in term time we were only home for our teas and just doing yard work. There were hens to feed and we generally kept a pig. You could use all of it except its squeal. You didn't buy chickens in those days, you hatched your own. We had a few sheep for a year or two, but we didn't keep them long. The hillside was all bracken then, you couldn't find them!

I left school when I was fourteen and I worked on our farm. We were at Riddings until I was sixteen years old, then my family went to live at Grange, taking over from a chap called Featherstone. I don't think he was related to the other Featherstones in Westerdale. There were a lot of Featherstones about! The same as Dowsons ~ there are a lot of Dowsons, but they're not all relations. Grange farm was twice as big as Riddings. I worked at home, at Grange, with my Dad.

Arthur

Now there are no cornfields in Westerdale, but in those days every farm had a few fields of corn, and we had to get a thresher. In war time they made you plough and sow corn, maybe more than some people wanted to. We had only horse drawn binders. In Dad's time everybody had a thresher of their own in a barn. But, when it got in a bigger way, there was one that came around the district, and we helped one another to have a day's threshing. When it first came round it was driven by a steam engine, but it had changed to a tractor machine before we ever got it. You'd need twelve or fourteen people working together to make the job easy, working on one farm at a time. You'd cut corn into sheaves, then build them into stooks in the fields. Then you would "hear the church bells twice" to dry them out in the stook before you laid them in haycocks, where they would be safe if they couldn't be led straight away and there was a showery day.

The rain would run off them, or if you did get a vicious rain then you'd have to tip them over and remake them. Combines didn't come in till much later. Not many grow corn now. There isn't a turnip or a potato field either. If you go over the moor there's quite a few turnip fields in Farndale because there they grow them for the sheep.

Hay wagon

96

This is actually Harry Thorpe being held aloft by Bob Cook and Martin Dowey on Castleton Cricket field, but Arthur must have had many proud moments just like this.

I didn't start to play cricket until I was sixteen years old. I joined Westerdale Cricket Club. The war meant that although we didn't lose a lot of players to the army, they left to go to work. A lot of them went to work on the railway at Middlesbrough and suchlike, and moved away. In wartime we were really short of players and had a job to get a team together. The 'Dales League' was the league at that time, from Ingleby to Grosmont, because you could get there on the train. We could go on the two o'clock train, and if you could get finished you'd get back at six. If you didn't you had to wait till nine o'clock. Bransdale and Rosedale came into the league much later.

Quoits finished in 1939, and restarted after the war. There was a pitch by Westerdale School Hill, but eventually it got covered over and never used any more. A lot of the farms had employed a young lad, taking them on when they were fourteen and they stayed till they were sixteen. Then a lot of them went to Lingdale into the pits, or into the works, where they'd get a better wage. The farms began doing without these youngsters. So it became difficult to find enough people to make up a quoits team.

During the war there was an army camp in one of Arkangel's fields, the one that John Hardisty has now, and there was a searchlight there. The Home Guard were out on a night, and they had an old car and you used to see them sitting in the car on a moor top watching for invaders ~ parachutes, and people coming from the coast. Tom Mortimer, Tom Bowes and Walter Wilson went to fight in the War, and Eleanor Hardisty was involved too.

The road up Sugar Loaf and the road through Hob Hole got an Army grant to be mended properly after the war, about 1950, because tanks had used those roads to go on the moors to practice. There must have been a bit of grouse shooting even in war time, because I remember being out on the moors above Eddie Muir's and

Joe Featherstone in the year that Westerdale won both the cricket and the quoits cup. When Westerdale played cricket at home Joe waited for the result and if they won he blew his hunting horn from the cricket field to let the village know.

seeing tanks stuck down the hillside with tracks off, one bogged down in the peat, and in over end into soft spots and sinking mud, where they'd been driving anywhere over the moor. They made deep holes full of water in the roads, and you could hardly ride a pushbike over Hob Hole.

We used to go to dances, and I can remember going over to one at Rosedale with George Mortimer. He had relations there and he took one or two of us over to the dance. I remember how bad the road was. It was only a rough road over Castleton and Blakey Rigg. It was humped up with a bit of stone down the middle and sloped away to ditches at either side by Ralph's Cross and along by the Blakey pub. It was difficult to get into Rosedale. The first part of Castleton Rigg was tarred in about 1930. Westerdale village street was tarred only to the top of the village, as far as the corner to Lead Lane. They did down Ossiker Crook bank to the bridge after we came, because it was washing out with water.

Arthur in Whitby

Me and Elsie met at a Christmas party in Farndale. Five or six of us made up a taxi load to go to the dance there. Alwyn Champion ran the taxi at that time. We met at that Christmas party, but I didn't see her again until August at the Farndale Show. We played cricket at Farndale and Elsie was scoring there ~ for us! She said she had to do something to stop me getting all those runs! Will Tinsley scored for Farndale. Mostly I used to use my push bike to go to Farndale, but one night I went over on a horse. The roads were bad and I couldn't go over any other way. I put it in Potter's stable till I wanted to go home. We got married in 1951 at Farndale Chapel, which is now a house, because it was on a 99 year lease and the lease ran out, and they couldn't renew it. We came back to live in Westerdale.

Arthur & Elsie married in November 1951

As soon as the war came we started to sell milk and it went away in cans, mostly shifted by motor wagons though it went on the train in bad weather. The Milk Board took it all and paid for it, and more farms in Westerdale took up milking when you could get it away. The milk was going to Driffield at that time to be made into dried milk. It used to go through a machine and come out like rolls of paper. Then it was crushed into powder.

You got the same price getting it away whether you were near or far from the dairy. Milk was more valuable in those days. But then later the bigger farms nearer the dairies wanted more money for their milk and they got the Milk Board stopped! That was the worst thing they ever did, because now the Milk Board has stopped, the supermarkets just pay what they want to, and they're not paying enough.

Cow cake and pig food cost only about £20 a ton but now it's £140 a ton. Things like that have gone up maybe four or five times their own value. But milk hasn't gone up four or five times its own value. As far as I can remember it was only about four pence a gallon when Bonuses were putting it on the train. But a hundred pound milk cheque back then was worth more than a thousand pound cheque is now. Because your cow cake bill is a lot bigger. A few years ago farmers were getting a hundred pounds a ton for corn. Now they're only getting about sixty pounds but the price of food hasn't come down. Also every time new regulations come out it's expensive to keep up with them. To start with you had your cow byres to put right. Then you had to build a milk house. Then you had to buy a refrigeration tank. It cost us £5,000 just to build a milking parlour. It's just been taken out now because it's not used. If you wanted to stay in milk you had to go on spending money. When we first went to Grange Farm we had just ten cows. By the time we finished at Grange Farm we were keeping forty, milkers and followers. We packed up ploughing and just grew hay by the finish, because we needed more grass.

Grange Farm Westerdale, in November 2006

It would have been the 1960s before everybody in Westerdale had milking machines. The first ones that came around were 'Hillman Simplex'. They could be run with petrol engines. We had one run on a petrol engine for quite a while before we got it run on electricity. For a while nearly every farm sold some milk, but now there is only one milk tanker coming to one farm in Westerdale.

For a long time in Westerdale we had our own water supply. It was ten bob a year to pay. It came from Spring Dyke by Blue Shales, the hill above Herbert Flintoft's. When they built the reservoir they didn't take Spring Dyke in, but used other springs from higher up. Sweet Banks up Esklets, and Stockdale feed it. Electricity came to Westerdale pretty soon after the War, but it was 1960 before it came round the farms. That was done with a Government grant. If everybody decided to have it done you could have it a bit cheaper. There weren't many telephones in Westerdale. Just the one in the Post Office and the telephone box.

There's a change in sheep farming too. Sheep wander a long way. When they get in the wrong place, nobody wants to own them. They take their teeth with them! It's surprising how far they'll walk in a night, just wandering slowly on, and until they're turned, they don't turn around and start coming back. When Marshfield had their sheep out on the Howe, Milner's sheep didn't go over there because there was a man there with a dog, but there aren't the shepherds now. Both those flocks have gone. Miss Ellerby hasn't any out now, nor Holly Lodge. Crag House hasn't any now nor Ken Willie Dowson. John Rudsdale's at Stormy Hall have gone. Potters and Honey Bee had some but haven't now. They're all gone. The moors will change. Even down Castleton there's long grass now. There's not enough sheep to eat it off.

Elsie ~

I came here from Farndale when we got married, in 1951. My Dad worked on the roads, and I grew up with my aunts and uncles, eight of them, who were like brothers and sisters. I went to Farndale school. There were more than a dozen evacuees there from Middlesbrough and from Hull, so we had two extra teachers. We were all in one school room!

We used to go to Castleton to the "Ernie Flintoft" Cricket Match in August, but I didn't come over this way for the Castleton Show. The roads were rough and there was no transport over the top.

Elsie (Ford in those days)

When I left school I did house work, and during the war I went to work on a milk farm at Stokesley, in the house and also washing milk bottles and bottling milk. Then I worked in forestry for five and a half years at Wykeham, part of Dalby Forest near Scarborough. Dalby Forest stretches almost from Rosedale to Scarborough. I was growing trees from seeds. We'd plant out a nursery bed, and have so many ounces of seed, for seven rows, I think it was, so long. You hadn't to put a lot in one spot, and not enough in another! There were sitka spruce and larch and so on ~ larch is not good because it's shallow rooted and won't stand the wind.

There are still the nursery beds out on the top there now. They were all set out in lines with the little trees in, and when the trees got to the right height they dug them up and planted them elsewhere. In the nurseries we weeded, and when the trees got so high we would "line them out". There were long pieces of wood about eighteen inches deep and they had notches in, and you would put a little tree in each notch, with another piece of wood alongside it to clamp them in. Then the lads would take them and bury their roots so they were growing in lines. After that we had to take them up and put them in bundles. For that job we were sometimes on piece work. We had to get a thousand trees and put them in bundles, hundreds or maybe two hundred and fifties. That was fun, on piece work. There were three of us in the team, two lasses and a lad. When I first started there were eight lasses, then five, then when I left to get married I was the last lass to leave, except for Em, who was the secretary in the office. I still write to her. They weren't employing girls in the team any more because lads were taking the jobs. One day we were doing piece work when a chap came up through the trees and said "How are you doing lasses? I'll just help you with a thousand!" We were all right ~ we could make what money we wanted! Well, you hadn't to make a lot of money, but you could make more than a day's pay. Some of those bundles were sent up to Scotland.

Elsie at work at Dalby Forest before she was married

I used to come home on a Saturday dinner time with my fingernails all worn off from pulling weeds out. In the winter when we couldn't do anything in the nurseries we went out into the forest, and 'brashed' ~ took all the branches off the forest trees as high as we could reach, so that you could walk underneath. They don't do that now. Afterwards the trees would be felled, and a lot of them in those days would go to be pit props, which are not needed nowadays. They don't have workers there now like we were, they do it all on contract. They're felling a lot of the trees up there now. They've grown to maturity since then. It'll be replanted, I suppose. Recently we went up to see, and a friend said, "Look, they've felled El-slitherum and you can see a house up there now that we've not seen for seventy years! There was a threshing machine in the barn when we last saw it." "El-slitherum" was his name for the rather steep hillside! When our friend's Dad started work in the forest, that was his first job, to cut bracken on that hill among all the little trees. The house we were looking at used to be a farmhouse. There was a fire there, and it was rebuilt as a bungalow. There was no water there ~ they used to drink rain water. They used to do the same at Easby. All the roofs would drain into big tanks. I worked in the forest up until I was married.

We got married in 1951 at Farndale Chapel, and later we had two children. When we were married we came to live first in Westerdale in the cottage above Eleanor Hardisty's.

With their first child

We were there for about eight years. Arthur's Aunty had the shop across the road, where Miss Ruff lives now, and she was poorly, and I had to look after the shop while she was away. Her sitting room had a great big fireside in it, and I asked if she would like a little fireside instead. She said she would, and that she would pay for it but that I should choose it and get it done. So we got Wetherills to put it in. I papered the sitting room and painted it. She was only back for thirteen weeks before she died. But she was pleased. She liked it.

While she was there I would go and do jobs for her. "Chop me a bit of kindling," she would say. Where there is now the garage was what she called the warehouse. She stored things in there, and there were boxes and pieces of wood. I was in there to chop kindling once and I was sitting down on a nice piece of wood when Dr Bob came in. "That's the well under there!" he said. I never sat there any more! I didn't know there was a well in the warehouse. Many of the farms down the village street once had wells ~ Church House, Town Farm and behind Doweys. At the bottom of the village they got water out of a trough in the Keeper's field. Arthur remembers that the well in Town Farm's yard worked in the 1940s when Holmes's were there. If the water was frozen they had to pump it out of the well for the beasts to drink. There was a well behind the church, and Hannah Mary Carr used to be given sixpence to carry water from there to the copper and wash and boil the church linen.

I remember when Mrs Edwards was the cook at Westerdale village school. She'd been to the village shop for some bread and there wasn't any. So she came to ask me if I had any spare. "I've made the children some soup, and I have no bread." I said I had a little loaf, but it was only a small one. She said "That'll do fine. Now cut a piece off first for your own meal." She wasn't going to leave me without a bite.

There was a time at Grange when I had a hen sitting on four goose eggs. A hen could only cover four to keep them warm. She 'forsaked' them. A hen only sits for three weeks and a goose egg needs four, so you don't know whether a hen will sit for the four weeks. So I took them to another "clucker" and left them in her nest box. Out came a little gosling, then another one. A little boy was visiting then, and I said "Are you coming with Elsie to see if there's another gosling?" He said yes, he would, and there was a third little gosling, then another one came out. Next day he said "Come on Essie, let's go and see if there's another little gosling." We had got four out, but I didn't know how we could get five goslings out of the four eggs!

Our son David was born in the cottage, but we were living at Grange by the time our daughter Valerie was born. I have great grandchildren now! I remember when a little friend of our Valerie's came to play. She was chasing David about, and he jumped on the muck midden. The little lass tried to do the same and she went in the muck! "Aunty Elsie," she said, "I didn't know it was sinking mud!" It was cow muck just swept off the yard. I had to pull her trousers off and swill them. Never mind, I got plenty of water at them, then a broom, then a brush and got them clean.

Elsie with David

There are at least sixteen new houses in Westerdale since I came here. There's the Blacksmith's shop converted, the Keeper's house, Dorothy Dowey's two, the top end of Duncombe House next to the Stanleys, Kestrel House, and the Darcy's two made from farm buildings, Wilden's stables, the Sanderson's in the coach house at the Hall, Mark and Alisons' house, Carr House has built another, Dale Side has split into two. Dale View Yard, and Broadgate's bungalow. They happened in a rush together, over this last twenty years. They had just started building the filter house when we were married. I don't know what they'll do with that now they've finished with it. When Valerie started school there was just John Hardisty and Alan Mould on the school bus, but now there are lots of children on it. The Youth Hostel has closed too. There have been a lot of changes.

Arthur & Elsie in 1973

102

A talk with Mrs Eleanor Hardisty of Westerdale in 2001

Mrs Hardisty said, "I was born at Town Farm in Westerdale. It was a proper working farm at that time, with cows, sheep, ducks and geese and turkeys to kill for Christmas. I had two sisters and four brothers, and I was the youngest but one ~ I had a brother who was younger than me. My Grandfather Ellerby worked in a wood yard at Easingwold, but he died when my father was young. I knew my Grandma on my mother's side."

Eleanor Ellerby (Hardisty) in 1931

Eleanor went to Westerdale School, and left when she was fourteen. She enjoyed school, and liked her teacher. Some of her brothers and sisters were there at the same time. She also went to the Sunday school sessions that were held after services in the Church, and then later were held in the Institute. The family didn't have holidays because they couldn't leave the farm, but Eleanor liked the summer times best. She enjoyed day trips to the sea side and they sometimes went to Castleton Show. At hay time Eleanor helped by making haycocks, when the hay that was laid loose on the fields was gathered up and made into haycocks, which were built into big stacks in the yards.

Mrs Ellerby, Eleanor's mother, at the door of Arkangel

"In my teens the family moved further up the village to Arkangel. My father had become very ill and was unable to carry on farming. Arkangel and the land around it belonged to my father, and Arkangel had been let. When the lady who had the let died we were able to move there. My sisters and I lived at home with our parents until we were married. Now, in 2001, I have just one sister left. Electricity was not installed in Arkangel when I was living there, and it wasn't installed in our present house until after our son John was born. I remember hanging a Tilley lamp up high once he was moving around so that he couldn't knock it over. We used oil lamps and candles, and reading in bed was impossible unless you had a good flash light!"

When Mrs Hardisty left school she worked at the Vicarage in Westerdale. Throughout the war one of her brothers worked Town Farm. Her brothers and sisters were not called up because they were working in farming, but Mrs Hardisty was called up in 1944 because she was not working in farming.

"I was in the ATS for three years. I joined up at Pontefract and for most of the time I served at Birkenhead, with a short time in Southport, and my main work was as a cook. I got a notification to join, and I had no choice about whether I should go, or to where, or in what I should do! I met some very nice people, though, and made a lot of friends. We young women lived in the barracks, in wooden hut-like buildings which I found were very comfortable. Birkenhead was a training camp for troops in the use of weapons. Tom Mortimer from Dale View in Westerdale was there for a while.

"I came back after the war to Arkangel, and I took over the Post Office. Officials from the Post Office came to help me to set it up when I began, and then they came occasionally to see if everything was all right." Eleanor, Miss Ellerby then, ran the Post Office from Arkangel for about a year, and then she married Bill Hardisty and when she moved back into the village with him she took the Post Office with her.

Joiners/blacksmith's shop for sale in 1992, by John Hardisty. Formerly owned by Feversham Estates

Eleanor met Bill when his family left Farndale to move to the house where she lives now, and his father took over the blacksmith's shop in Westerdale from Mr Kemp. Bill Hardisty was born in Farndale, when his father was the blacksmith then, and Bill helped his Dad. Bill's mother died, and after they came to Westerdale his father married the village schoolteacher, Miss Watson. Bill's father moved with his new wife to Bainbridge and the blacksmith's shop closed. Bill stayed in Westerdale. Bill's brother was not a blacksmith ~ he lived in Castleton for while, then went to be a gardener and chauffeur at Upsall Hall near Ormesby Bank. During the war Bill was in the Artillery in France, and they waited until the war was over for the wedding. They had a church wedding in Westerdale with a reception in the School Hall. Eleanor Ellerby became Eleanor Hardisty, and was married in a lovely long white satin dress. After the war Bill was a farmer.

Mrs Hardisty remembers the annual dance in aid of Whitby Hospital, and there was a Fancy Dress Ball in the winter, with a dance and a supper. Bill played cricket, and quoits. There was a quoits pitch on the grass at the bottom of School Hill. There were whist drives. Eleanor did a lot of knitting. Her mother was a good matter (clip mats and hooky mats) and Eleanor matted too.

Bill Hardisty's brother Ian

Their son John was born in 1950. The village school closed in 1954, so he had to go to Castleton to school. Derrick Champion had a taxi and used to do the school run. Even when Mrs Hardisty was a child Champions were running a taxi service. She remembers when there were no cars, and transport was a train or a pony and trap. There were no tractors, and horses were used for farm work ~ ploughing, hay time, harvest. She also remembers the first car in Westerdale, at Church Farm.

Mrs Hardisty took the Post Office over from the two Miss Featherstones, Frances and Emma, when they retired. They had first run it from Ivy Holme, and then they moved it to Rose Cottage which they had built. Eleanor says she can remember the building of Rose Cottage, with an additional small building put on the side especially to house the Post Office. When she was at school she and the other children used to stand and watch the builders at dinner time. Rose Cottage is one of a pair of brick built houses, where Mary Mortimer lives now.

Clippy Rug Group

In the days when the Miss Featherstones had the Post Office the mail came from Whitby to Castleton by train, was sorted there, then brought by the postmen in big mail bags over to Westerdale. The Post Office (a sub-office) dealt with pensions, stamps, and savings. When it was moved from Arkangel to the village centre there was more business. There were a lot of hikers and hostellers who came in, especially on Saturday mornings. People staying at the Youth Hostel overnight came in for stamps for their postcards. The Post Office was open six days a week in those days, 9am~4pm, and 9am~12pm on Saturdays.

The Post Office couldn't be left unattended, and the hours Mrs Hardisty worked meant she found the visiting trade vans specially welcome. The butcher used to come round with his horse drawn cart at one time, and there was a baker and a greengrocer. Mr Scarth the grocer would come calling as well, with his van on a Thursday morning. Washing and general housework had to be fitted around customers, and shopping had to be done out of Post Office hours.

Mrs Hardisty had to keep quite a bit of money in her Post Office, but she never had any hold-ups! She dealt with Postal Orders, valued from a shilling, or now 5p, up to a pound when she first started. Stamps were of one "class", with no first and second class. There were penny stamps. There was more mail than there is nowadays. Without telephones people relied on letters. Post cards were used for short messages.

"I didn't sell post cards, but Castleton Post Office did. Post cards were sold at the Westerdale village shop, where Miss Ruff lives. I remember they only cost a penny. There were more parcels, mainly for birthdays and specially at Christmas, both arriving and being sent, because there were no delivery vans then, like there are now, so they all came by post. There was only one delivery, and at first there was no evening collection. The postman used to collect the mail from here at dinner time.

"When I first started the post all came in a mail van from Whitby in the morning. The local sorting office was in Castleton, and telegrams came by way of Castleton, not Westerdale. Mr Medd and his wife, the parents of the present postmaster Mr David Medd, were in charge of Castleton Post Office then. A postman from Castleton delivered letters in Westerdale village, and to Hall Farm and the Mill. He used to walk to do his round. There were two postmen then, with Mr Peacock and also Mr Gray who did all round the outside of the dale, and up Woodend. He started along Daleside and then went back up to Broadgate. Up Woodend, and in those days he had to go up to Esklets if they had post, to where a family lived who farmed sheep. There was some good land up there at one time, but it's gone back to the moor now. Mr Gray was supposed to walk, but he used to bring his own bike, and use that. Mr Gray would come in to see me at dinner time to get any mail that I had collected up to then, and he would put it on the two o'clock train to Whitby.

"Then in later days the night postman came after four o'clock, just before closing time, to collect the rest.   He wouldn't stay in Westerdale long ~ he'd be in a hurry because he had to get round all the post offices all the way down the valley, Castleton, Danby, Lealholm, Egton, right down to Whitby, to collect. Nowadays the Danby men collect all around the post boxes, and come here just before half past four, and take the mail into Whitby in the van. Then a post van goes from Whitby to York, taking what there is, and collecting what's to come back.

"When I first started I didn't much deal with pensions, but when that really began and more people were coming in, it made more work for the Post Office. There were quite a few people collecting them then, but Linda who now runs Westerdale Post Office hasn't many.   A lot of people get their money paid into the bank nowadays."

The Westerdale Post Office was in Mrs Hardisty's care for forty~six and a half years. She would have liked to have made it to fifty years, but had to give it up in 1994 when her husband Bill became ill, and she needed to look after him.

Mrs Eleanor Hardisty, Westerdale Postmistress from 1948, at her counter in the hallway of her cottage in Westerdale just before she retired in 1994

Reminiscing with Mrs Mary Mould of Westerdale, 2001

Mary Mould, who was Mary Dale, was born in 1921 at Quarry Farm in Westerdale. Her father, George, was born at High House in Westerdale in 1888, where his father was at that time a tenant farmer. George got work on a farm when he left school at thirteen. He worked at Dale View for a time, and also at Carr House where Mrs Topham now lives for some people called Pennock. Then he worked on the roads for the council ~ he was a road man. Mary's mother was Lucy Hartley, sister to Mary, David, Hannah, Martin and Beatrice (who was Emma Beeforth's mother).

Mary explained that in those days, when she was a small child, there were not always enough houses available in Westerdale. So for a while she and her mother lived with her Hartley Grandparents at Quarry Farm, whilst her father and her sister Greta, two years older than Mary, stayed with her father's parents, who by then were living at Westerdale Mill. The Mill was still working at that time, and her Grandfather milled corn for the local farmers. Later Mary's uncle, her Dad's brother, took over the mill, but Mary doesn't remember whether it was still working then. Then her Grandparents went to live at a place called Priestcroft, near Skelton. Then back to Westerdale, and after that they retired to a cottage in Castleton.

Mary (right) with her sister Greta in 1931

Mary, her sister and her parents came to live together in 1923, in the cottage where she still lives, when Mary was two years old. Her Grandfather Dale died on Christmas Eve in 1932, and her Grandfather Hartley the following March, three months later. But they both had their Golden weddings.

All of Mary's school days were spent at Westerdale. She didn't enjoy any of the subjects very much, but she did like the playground games, of hopscotch, skipping and rounders. Mary used to come home for her dinner, but children from the outlying farms brought their own packed lunch. Nothing to eat was provided by the school. School time was from 9m till 3.30pm with an hour's break at mid~day. She left when she was fourteen.

In the summer Mary enjoyed going to nearby Agricultural Shows at Danby and Castleton, and a little one at Commondale. The school children entered the handwriting competition class. She remembers going to Commondale school to do her writing. There were Sunday School trips by bus from Westerdale to Whitby and sometimes Scarborough or Saltburn. They would spend all day on the sands unless it rained, when they would see the entertainments or go to the pictures. They ate ice creams, and there were donkeys to ride, though Mary wasn't very keen on donkey riding. Mary's cousin Emma Beeforth tells of the time when as children she and Mary's older sister Greta "borrowed" the neighbour's donkey and put Mary and William, Emma's little brother, on its back for a ride. It wouldn't walk, so Emma and

Eddie & Alan Jackson riding on donkeys at the bottom of Bobbies Bank, Danby.

Greta pulled its tail. Instead of walking it bucked the two little ones off! Much crying went on, and Emma and Greta were in trouble with their elders. They were sent to their rooms.

Mary didn't have summer holidays away, except for visits to her mother's family at Quarry Farm which were very enjoyable. In the summer Greta and Mary might stay there with their Grandparents, Aunts, and cousins Emma and William for as long as a month. Sometimes they helped with activities on the farm, though Mary says she wasn't much of a hand at making haycocks. She liked riding in the wagon, "Now you bairns, sit down at' bottom!" the men would say to them, as the horse and empty wagon went down to re-load. The home-made ginger beer was good! And baskets and baskets of cakes. In the pantry at Quarry Farm there was always plenty to eat.

A horse rake

At Christmas they might stay at Quarry Farm for a week, and there was a big family gathering, especially since it was Grandfather William Hartley's birthday on Christmas Day. One Christmas when Mary wasn't very old she found a bowl of butter and rum that someone had left to warm to make the rum sauce to go with the Christmas pudding, and she ate it. She slept all afternoon. After tea on Christmas day each year all the grandchildren were presented by Grandfather with a shilling, and the family gathered round the piano for singing and music. Mary didn't play the piano, but liked singing. The Aunts and Uncles liked singing, and Mary remembers how one night the carol singers came in to their cottage and had such a rousing song session round their piano there. Her father didn't think he had a good voice, so he used to go with the carol singers as "cadger", with the collection box. The Methodist choir used to come round too.

Early on Christmas morning the children would go round the houses and "shout", being "the Lucky Bird", knocking on the doors, taking greenery in and calling Happy Christmas. They would be given perhaps a penny each and probably some cake. The children would be laden down with cake. They couldn't eat it at every house or they would be sick! Mary didn't go with them, but her Mother always liked the Lucky Bird to come on Christmas morning, and wouldn't let anyone go out or come in till the Lucky Bird had been to bring them good luck. As a child Mary looked forward very much to Christmas, and to Father Christmas, though there was never very much in the children's stockings. Maybe a book or a game, an orange or an apple. Her Dad would go into Castleton on Christmas Eve to the shop there to buy the presents for the girls. Mary was very sad when she found out it was him, as she'd believed so much in Father Christmas.

When Mary was little she always liked dolls and she can remember going shopping with her Mum and her Aunt Hannah to Loftus. There was a shop window there,

Mary Dale (Mould) in 1934

displaying rows and rows of dolls. Mary would have loved to have one of the big ones. She didn't get one, but her mother did buy her a doll - one of the little ones. She called him Alan! Mr Hardisty, the Westerdale blacksmith who lived next door, made her a cradle for her dolls out of a horse shoe nail box. Her Mother made the cradle some bedclothes. She didn't get pocket money, but occasionally they were given pennies to buy sweets at the shop across the road.

Before the Hardistys came to live next door a Mr Kemp lived there, and he was the blacksmith in Westerdale before Bill Hardisty's father was. Mary is still in touch now occasionally with Mr Kemp's son Ronald, who was a Methodist preacher. Herbert Flintoft's parents lived at Lieth House where the Thompsons live now. When she was very little the Miss Featherstones who had the post office then, where Emma lives now, took Mary there for tea, and to see new baby Bessie Flintoft. Mary took one of her dolls, which was dressed in velvet. The grown-ups asked her what she called her doll. "Bessie Flintoft, of course!" answered Mary! The Miss Featherstones would do anything for anyone, she says. They helped her when her mother died.

Emma's mother, Mary's Aunt Beattie, made coats from adults' cast offs for Greta, Emma and Mary, who had only a year's difference in age between each of them. Mary remembers lots of hand-me-down clothes coming her way.

Emma and Mary remember that when they were teenagers the young people from all around would congregate in Castleton to chat together by the fish and chip van when it visited each Saturday night. It was owned by a local man ~ Matty Pearson. Then they all would meet again for church on Sunday night. They sat on the back pews. After church the young lasses went for a walk along the lanes, and then there were the lads following a few paces behind! Mary enjoyed the village dances and social events, and she did some embroidery. As a teenager she went to afternoon sewing classes,

"School House" is the cottage at the end, with" Ivyholme" to the right.

followed by embroidery classes, in Temperance Hall, now the Village Hall, in Castleton. Mary made a dress or two at her sewing class. The young ladies wore hats and gloves to go to church and for special occasions, and Mary liked to try to get a new hat for Easter. Hats could be bought in Whitby.

There was no television ~ and at first no wireless. The first wirelesses were accumulator battery ones. The heavy batteries had to be carried to Castleton to be charged at Champions. The first wireless that Mary's family had was hand made by Mr Esmarch, who used to live in Ivy Cottage next door to Mary, before Emma lived there. He was a traveller in electrical goods, who had lived at Burton Leonard, near Harrogate.

When Greta, Mary's sister, left school she went to work as a waitress at the Moorlands Hotel. Not long after Mary left school her mother took on the job of school cleaner, and Mary helped her. The school teacher always lived in School House, the other side of Emma's cottage. There was a Miss Dent there in 1926, and at one time there was a Mrs Emmitt. Mary's mother's health wasn't very good so Mary didn't go far away, and did most of the school caretaker job herself. Twice a day they went in, and in winter they were there very early to light the stove and the open fire to make the room warm for the children. Her father helped by emptying the earth closets.

Mary began courting with Robert (she says he's a "quarter cousin") in 1937 when she was about 16. Robert Hodgson Mould, Mary's husband to be, was born at Bagdale in Westerdale in 1915. His mother's maiden name was Hodgson. His father was a farmer, and he had several brothers and sisters. For a time Robert's school teacher was Mary's Aunt Hannah. Robert's family moved to Danby Dale in 1921 when he was six years old. After that they lived at Howe Farm in Castleton. When he left school Robert was a general farm worker, working in Fryup and Danby. In 1939 he went to work at one of the farms at Baysdale Abbey for Lord Boynes as a shepherd.

During the war those who were working the farms were not asked to go and fight. Robert did not leave his farm work, and Emma Beeforth was also not required to go away to do war work because she was working at Hall farm. But Mary had to go in front of a tribunal to see whether she should. She didn't want to go away to do war work because of her mother's poor health, but that wasn't considered a sufficient reason. She failed a medical test, however. Mary thinks it was because she has some toenails and finger nails missing. She had them till she was eight years old, but then lost them, and remembers having her hands wrapped in bandages for weeks. Their doctor called in another doctor to see her because he'd never seen anything like it. Nobody could say why it happened.

Mary had a live-in job for part of each week for some years in the forties at Crown House on the valley side above Westerdale cricket ground, where she helped with the Dixon's household and their young family. (Mrs Dixon's son later married Mrs Grace Hardy's daughter, and the Hardy parents moved here from Birmingham to look after Mrs Dixon who was by then elderly and would otherwise have been alone here when her son married and left home. Now, in 2001, Grace is living alone at Crown House.)

Mary was working at Crown House during the war when a bomb was dropped on the moor just their side of Hob Hole, making a large crater. Mary and Mrs Dixon had planned that in the event of an air raid they would take care of a child each (there were two at that time). That night when the bomb fell the house shook, bringing the soot down the chimneys, and they rushed with the children to go downstairs. Another bomb dropped near Riddings farm. Mary thinks the search light at Archangel attracted them.

During the war Mary called at houses around the village and a few further afield each week and collected money in exchange for National Saving Stamps. The scheme was devised to help the war effort. Mary still has a list of those who subscribed. She would give them stamps in exchange for money, and

"Crown House", Westerdale

people would stick the stamps on a card. When they had enough they could exchange them for Savings Certificates at the Post Office. Mary herself was presented with a certificate, thanking her for "Notable Service from 1943 to 1945", for collecting the National Savings.

At one time Mr and Mrs Dixon, and Mrs Dixon's parents Mr and Mrs Lumb, exchanged houses ~ they lived in Barker Road in Middlesbrough. Every month Mary went on the bus from Castleton to stay there for a week, from Monday to Friday. She went to clean, and to look after the children. Mary also worked for Major and Mrs

A cup victory for Westerdale. The team is:
Back left to rt:) Henry Thompson, Robert Mould, Charles Hartley, Reuben Johnson, Alfred Mould, (Middle) Robert Cook, William Hardisty,
(Capt. with cup) Martin Dowey, Leggy Wood,
(Front) Harry Thorp, George Booth.

Blakeborough at their house on Westerdale Side for a while in the late forties. She went for one or two half days each week. Miss Haycroft and Miss Gerund lived there before the Blakeboroughs, and when the sale of the house and contents was held Mary's Aunt Beattie took her to meet the Blakeboroughs, and they gave her a job then, scrubbing out, and she stayed on to clean each week. Mrs Blakeborough was very nice, but she didn't see the Major very often. He was always in his study. She wasn't allowed in there to disturb the papers and books which were from floor to ceiling right round the room, in case anything got mislaid.

Robert was working at Baysdale from 1939. He "lived in" with the farm manager, Mr Close. He did not get much spare time, usually working long hours, gathering the sheep over large areas of moor, and in the spring bringing some of them to the "intakes", more sheltered fields adjoining the moor, for lambing. But he used to come as often as he could, perhaps two or three times a week, from Baysdale to Westerdale to visit Mary.

There are two ways to come ~ one is over the rough moor, and then there's another better track by way of Hob Hole. The moor way is the quicker one and there is a legend that Robert built a bridge over a stream on the moor so that he could visit Mary more easily. Mary says she would probably have known about the bridge at the time, but she'd completely forgotten the story till the vicar mentioned it at Robert's funeral in January 2000. After a while he got a horse, so he could ride to visit her, instead of walking. He owned a few horses through his life. He got a bike, then a motor bike, but that didn't last long. She has a photograph of Robert, on the bridge.

Mary says he was always laughing, was Robert.

The bridge in 2005

Reminiscing with Mrs. Mary Mortimer of Westerdale in 2001.

Mary's maiden name was Mould, and she was born in Westerdale in 1917 in Bagdale House. Mary had eight brothers including Robert, and one sister. She said.....

Mary in 2006

"My Grandfather Hodgson farmed at Ainthorpe Farm, the biggest farm in Danby at the time, which belonged to the Ness -Walkers of Whitby. They were at one time either very good friends, or distant relatives of the Hodgson family. My mother, Sarah Anne Hodgson who was born soon after 1880, served as a cook next door at the big house (which became the home of Dr Armstrong who came from Whitby and later was Dr Bob Robinson's house). She was the middle one of a family of five ~ four daughters and one son, who inherited.

My Grandmother Mould was called Mary Dowson, and she was the eldest of twelve at Falcon Farm, Danby. Lord Boynes, who for a lot of the summer came to live at Baysdale Abbey, needed someone to do dairy work ~ seeing to the milk, making the butter and milking the cows. Lady Boyne herself came across to Danby and saw the family, and chose the eldest, Mary Dowson who was just turned twelve years old at the time. She went across to Baysdale Abbey one Sunday with her belongings in a blanket box, and her next two younger brothers, who wouldn't be that old, went with her to carry the box. She settled in at Baysdale Abbey. Lady Boyne, whose husband was brother to Princess Mary, was impressed with her, and later asked her if she would stay and look after the children as well, so she went back to Branspeth Castle with them. In 1861 Mary Dowson, my grandmother, was married in St. Margaret's Church in Durham, and the Boynes attended, and gave her the wedding. My Grandfather Mould was an Inspector of Mines in the Durham area. Later, mainly because my grandmother was one of a family of twelve, my father had seventy cousins!

Builders of Botton Hall

My father was Robert Mould who came from Durham in 1900. He was training there to become an architect and had nearly come to his final year when his father died, and there were no means for him to carry on his training. During his training he'd done some work at Cragside in Northumberland in the 1890s. So he came to this area, and served an apprenticeship of seven years with Mr John Brown, the stonemason, who lived at Hill Garth in Westerdale.

He learnt first how to cut stone at a quarry, through every aspect of stone work. Eventually he helped to build Botton Hall in Danby Dale. He built the outbuildings and servants' quarters, and worked on sills and heads on the main house. He walked there to work from Bagdale House to Botton Hall every day in all weathers, and the wife of the owner of the house asked him to build her a summer house in the grounds. It is still there today, only sadly neglected. It is stone built, pine lined and pantiled, and faces to the south, as sun houses do.

"My parents were married in 1905, and they lived in Castleton in Piper Cottage, which belonged to Kitching's big grocery, drapery and animal meals shop in Castleton. The Kitching's son got married and needed the cottage so my parents weren't in it for very long, though just enough time to have two children born there. They heard about Bagdale House coming empty ~ one half already was and the other soon would be empty, so they moved to Arkangel, to wait for Bagdale to be ready.

"My family came to live in Westerdale in about 1907. They lived at Arkangel for about a year, waiting for Bagdale House to be empty so they would be able to there. During that year, 1908, their third child was born in the biggest snow storm that ever blew. There were three years between the first and the third child. They had nine children, and three of the boys' birthdays were nearly on the same day ~ 25th or 26th of February! They were Thomas, Annie and Frank.

One little girl is Hannah Mary Carr sitting in front of Bulmer's Monument, at Arkangel, Westerdale, around 1910

"Bagdale House was formerly two houses, and when my parents rented it from a man called Mr. Nicholson they made it into one house. That meant that for the growing family they had a lovely place because it was quite big. It had four bedrooms, two little pantries, and two back rooms in which to do the general washing up and that sort of work. There was no bathroom, of course, in those days. There were two front rooms, but no place to do the clothes washing. So the first thing my parents did was to build a wooden wash house, because they already had three children and therefore a lot of washing to be done. Then John, Alfred, Robert, and me, Mary, were born at Bagdale House. Our family loved Bagdale House. I can still remember the lamp on the table at Bagdale.

"I have vivid memories of living in Bagdale House although I was only three and a half when we left. My memory takes me back a long way, almost to the time of the First World War. As a child, of course, I didn't realise much about the War, but I was aware that the people around me were all so very busy and hardworking. Everybody seemed to be in working attire when I came the short distance down into the village from where I lived.

My father was a great gardener, and, coming from Durham, he grew leeks. We could always have fresh vegetables cooked straight from the garden. We had hens, so there were eggs to use, the clockers were put to hatch others, and the cockerels made a roast. There was a pig or two to feed. A pig to kill and cure was a good standby for any family. We had our own bacon. We had a few sheep, and killed our own lamb. If people had spare meat they sold it to their neighbours. We had two Shorthorn cows, so there was plenty of milk. In between all those jobs there was hay time to think about. So we were brought up plain, but wholesome.

Down at the bottom of the garden was a lovely little stream. There was a trough with water coming in and then out, and I can remember going down the little steps and playing. My brothers' favourite game was to play in the jet mines in the field. They got balls of string, and would go into the jet holes as far as they could. When my parents discovered what they were doing they were horrified. They immediately got some helpers to come from the village to help fill in the entrances. The boys could easily have got down the holes, such a long way with the length of string, had the tunnel fall in on them, and never been seen again. When they became bigger and bolder they were allowed to play on Sugar Loaf, and they used to catch Uncle John Featherstone's tup, and have a good ride around the hill on him!

John Featherstone from Church Farm was an unmarried man, but was always known as Uncle John. He was very tall, as strong as a horse, with a long beard. He had sheep rights to keep sheep on the moors, and a right to cut turves. He was cousin to Joe, Frances and Emma. I was once later told by a daughter of the family who came to visit that there were twelve Featherstones reared at Church Farm, and the only way to bake the bread there was on the hearth stone. There wouldn't have been twelve at home all at one time, of course, because in those days children were away to go to work at thirteen or fourteen. Uncle John Featherstone was the first in Westerdale to have a car. When he went to Castleton he couldn't reverse very well, so he went round by the Station to get home! That was before the first World War. During the First World War my father was a Police Special, and he was nearly always out at night. Then he lived long enough to be a Special in the Second World War!

Hill Garth right, with Church Farm left. Old vicarage beyond. Frances Featherstone left, Eliza Featherstone, Ruth Bowes & Tom Bowes her grandfather, husband of Abigail Featherstone.

Groceries came to the village by horse and cart ~ sometimes two horses pulling a wagon ~ so supplies were delivered to the door from Castleton. There were plenty of shops in Castleton in those days. There was a big shop where Champions Garage petrol pumps are now, known as the High Shop, where there were Quakers living. There was the Home and Colonial Stores, which is now the Co~operative, and then another at the bottom on the corner to Ashfields which was Kitchings shop. It was a very big store, selling everything! Nobody went to town to shop, so you could buy your shoes and your corsets and your hair ribbons, and every mortal thing you wanted! The shops were there right through the twenties and thirties, even the forties. Things changed after the war. Transport became easier.

When the family needed a doctor, Dr English came all the way from Sleights in his car. He was an up and coming modern doctor ~ the best in the Esk Valley. His father, Dr Thomas, was there before him. Dr Armstrong hadn't yet come to Danby, and although there was Dr Jack in Castleton he hadn't done his training. Guisborough was the next nearest. It was difficult to get word to Dr English if he was needed in a hurry. Perhaps they sent a letter on the train. He came up once because four or five of the children all had measles at once. Mother used the sitting room for a sick room with the fire on to keep it aired, and Dr English said they were all to do as they were told, and stay in there with the curtains shut, and they did, and they didn't come to any harm.

Dr Jack Alexander

While my father lived at Bagdale he took on what was known as a "butter badger" business. He went around farms and bought up the butter, eggs, rabbits, and anything else that was going, and then went over into Cleveland on a certain day and had a door to door trade, to sustain his family. Because by then my mother needed a bit of help, and one of the Miss Featherstones, either Frances or Emma, would go and help her a day or two a week, because she had a big family. There were the cows to milk, when my father was at work, and the milk to set up and butter to make. Mother used to go round the bowls of milk with a piece of chalk, and mark them up. "Sn" meant Sunday night. "Sat n" for Saturday night and "Mm" for Monday morning. Milk was left standing in the cool dairy for three meals. The dairy floor was stone, there were stone slab shelves, and

Lisa Emma Featherstone

115

the window was covered with gauze to keep flies out. Friday night's milk would be done on Sunday morning, when the cream would be taken off with the creamer, which was like a big candlestick with holes in, and the cream would stay at the top, and the milk run through the bottom. The milk went out for the calves and the pigs.   And the cream was made into butter. We didn't have a separator in those days but when we got one much later I thought it was wonderful. The milk shot out of one spout and the cream out of another! There was plenty to be done.

There was no electricity, and the only drinking water we had was in a well across the field, so the water had to be carried, kept clean and covered with muslin in buckets for drinking. The children would have little buckets and whatever else they could get to carry the drinking water because my mother was not always able to leave the house to go across the field. There was a door on the well, leading to steps down to the water, and I can remember the older children, when I was a tiny tot, sending me back up the steps and telling me to stay at the top in case I fell in. But I had ventured down to have a look, and the water was ice cold. My mother used to spring clean it when she was spring cleaning the rest of the house ~ she cleaned it, washed it, scrubbed it ~ that was a day's work! While my parents were living at Bagdale the water was piped to the village. It came from Spring Dyke up past Broadgate below Blueshale and Otterhills and the tarn, and was piped to the reservoir above the cattle grid. It was lovely soft water.

Mother used to take us all to ride on a flat trap pulled by a horse to the station at Castleton, to take the train to Whitby in the holidays. That was always a highlight. We used to look in the jet shop windows, mainly in Church Street but there were others, and see them all working. They were carving out beautiful little pieces of jewellery, with very fine, sophisticated tools, and they never seemed to notice anybody looking in.   My parents bought me a jet brooch with Mary on, that I've still got. We went on the beach, and had a picnic. There were no fish and chip shops then ~ they were unheard of. I have a photograph that Mother had taken in Whitby of the first five children. They all had curls, specially the lads! We would get back exhausted at the end of a long day on the beach, and ride on the flat cart home again.

During the shooting season, (one for pheasant and one for grouse), the Lords of the Manor, Colonel Duncomb and all his entourage ~ family, friends and servants ~ came in their chariots from Helmsley to Westerdale Hall, their Shooting Lodge. The ladies of the village were invited to come down to the Hall any evening after dinner to have what was left over from the dinner table. Mother would take a basin, and she used to bring bits for the dogs, or for the hens, or maybe dripping, or some suet to make suet dumplings and puddings.   My sister remembered going with her, going in the back way, with the basin. Mother always brought something back.

Colonel Duncomb, ladies and dog outside Westerdale Hall

My sister could remember Westerdale flour mill working too. People took meal to be ground up, sometimes for flour, or sometimes for animals. My sister, who was born in 1907, remembered going with her mother, just the two of them, for Sunday evening supper with the Dale family at the Mill, and Mr Dale being very apologetic because the mill was working on a Sunday. He had a lot of work stacked up, lots of corn waiting to be done, and he had to set it going because people would be coming for it with their horses and carts.

When we lived in Westerdale we could go to the village where there was some activity, especially the Sunday School, and the Church and Chapel. There was a quoits club, and the cricket was well established. While he was living in Westerdale well before the War my father got permission to have a cricket field and formed a club. He had sons of his own to play, and the households then had a lot of people in them. There were lots of families of tens, eights, and sevens and so on, and there was often a cottage attached to a house where there were people living who were employed on the farms. There was horse work then, and hard work.

Mother often said that when she lived at Bagdale she was never lonely, because the people from the six farms up in Wood End and Esklets all came past the door where the foot path passed in front of the house, and they all called. In later years after they left the path was moved to the back of the house to come out near Arkangel gate. Now, of course, it's almost disappeared. There was a family called Cockerills who lived in Pinfold. Part of Pinfold was the storage for the estate workmen's equipment, and the family lived in the other part. They were a big family. When Mother went outside to hang the washing, all the nappies and so on, sometimes she could hear the Cockerill family like a choir of angels ~ they were such lovely singers. They had all the parts. They wouldn't know she was listening, because they were all sitting on the wall, singing. Mother said it was just lovely! Evelynne, who sings now at our chapel, is the daughter of one of them.

A later generation - Bill Cockerill

Then we moved on, to a farm in Danby Dale, to get employment for, and to find more money, to sustain the family. In the beginning of April 1921, when number eight, William, was expected in the May, my family and my father's brother's family exchanged houses, and we went to live in Plum Tree Farm in Danby Dale. It was all done in one day. I still remember the vast number of people who came to help to move us. All the village families and their men turned out to help, and there was a long trail of horses and carts. I can remember them taking my iron framed bed, where I slept with my sister. They put the feather pillows and the jerry pot in the middle and the feather bed and blankets round them, then a great big sheet over and tied it in a bundle and they put it on top of the cart! All the beds and furniture had to be loaded, and all the stuff from the dairy to do with the milk. Pot bowls galore, used for bread, for baking, or for setting the milk up. We had to have steady loads, well tied up, to take up and over the moor. When the line of wagons came to turn the corner round to Lead Lane old Mrs Crudas, from the middle cottage where the Taylors live now, dressed up in all her beads (she'd been a tenant at the Buck Inn in Castleton), came rushing out and gave me a little basket full of lovely sweets. I rode along on that cart feeling like the Queen. I thought it was exciting, as all things new are, but I soon found that it wasn't so exciting, going to a more remote place to live.

My mother told me that every one of her children couldn't wait to go to school. We all ran away to go there before we were old enough, and had to be hunted for. It wasn't far to go when we were in Westerdale, but in Danby Dale it was two miles, and we didn't always get there. I went to Danby School from Plum Tree, for nine years. We all loved school, and quite a lot passed tests for grammar school, but with the expense of the train, uniforms, books and so on, we couldn't afford it. It was too much. After I left school I stayed at home, helping.

My sister went to work at the Children's Home at Danby. There were sometimes twenty-five children there. They were sickly children who came from Middlesbrough on the train and stayed for a fortnight. One batch would be taken back to the station after the two weeks, and another batch collected. It was remarkable how well they did in that fortnight, with the fresh air, with plenty of good food, plenty of space to play around in, and well looked after. People around had an abundance of vegetables and everything which was good and fresh went to the Children's Home for the children's dinners. They loved their dinners. They were taken for walks, and they played games, and they had a play area at the back of the big house. All the washing was done two or three times a week, with the copper and the poss tub. My sister said the washing was a colossal job, with lines and lines of it. The Davidson Home was set up by the Davidson family, with a body of people from Middlesbrough who built it specially for its purpose, before I could remember. It went on in use for many years. They employed someone to look after the children, someone in the kitchen, a Matron and someone to help with the washing and work. There were very moderate wages because it was run as a trust. The Nancarols of Castleton Station did a lot for it, and the Punch's family of Ellerstang grew a lot of vegetables, to save them buying things. Most people helped. At Howe Wath we had a Siberian crab apple tree and we made more jelly with the fruit than we could use, and the children at the Home had custard with Siberian crab apple jelly turned out of little moulds in the centre of their plates. We took rhubarb for them as well. They had plain food, but it was wholesome and they did very well on it. Some were from very poor homes. People took spare clothing too. Up in Glaisdale there was a big house where some of their mothers could go. We called it "A Home For Tired Mothers"! But of course it isn't there now. My sister Annie worked at the Davidson Home for quite a while, then she "filled in" if one of the others took a break. She got married at 28, and lived away after that.

And then I came back to Westerdale. In 1933 we'd moved to Howe Wath, at Castleton. Howe Wath was a farm, so my father was a stonemason for part of the time, and a farmer the rest. Then before the Second World War my eldest brother Thomas took New House, with my next brother Frank. They rented it and were "on their beam ends", to begin with, because there was everything to buy. They

Distant New House, middle right, from Sugarloaf in 2005

had to take sheep there, and they needed cows, horses, carts and equipment. We hadn't been there very long when somehow my brother Thomas acquired a hen house, and we got fifty pullets in, and that was very good because the money for the eggs bought food. You gathered the eggs, cleaned them, and put them in the egg box. Then on a certain day during the week an egg collector came up Wood End on the main road. So one of us took our eggs across to Dale Side Farm, where the Merryweathers lived then. We carried the eggs in a proper egg box. There were trays in it, carrying thirty dozen eggs altogether, and it had two metal bands on the top that you slid a stick through to carry it by. We had to hold onto it, because we had to cross a stream by a tree trunk. We must have been fairly good on our feet, and strong!

I walked two or three times a week all the four or five miles from Howe Wath to New House to help them there. It was 1938, and I was 21 years old. I cooked for them, and I used to call at the shops and the butchers and carry everything to New House on my back. I also had to carry my gas mask! One day I had such a load I left it behind, and that evening on my way past Westerdale Hall there was a big iron gate which gave a big clank as I came through, and somebody jumped out from beside it. It was the policeman! "Where is your gas mask?" he said, and I hadn't got it with me. So I had to make sure I'd got it from then on, just in case. I put it in the bin after the war, I was so fed up with it!

Westerdale Hall

Sometimes my mother would visit my brothers and perhaps stay for a week, which she enjoyed. On the days I went to New House I would set off early in the morning, maybe in the dark, and arrive early and work all that day. When I got there I would put the side oven on, which had a fire of its own. That took quite a while to heat up to get a dinner ready. During the week I packed up all their washing and brought it back home to Castleton to do, because they didn't have a copper. Also I would prepare a meal for them to get themselves the next day, because I couldn't be there every day.

Mary

I had other jobs to do, going out to work, cleaning and scrubbing for a shilling a day. I would get back home to Howe Wath at about 7.30pm, and then often I would go on to a house in Ainthorpe where they took in visitors, and do all the washing up from a three course meal for about eighteen visitors. We had to make the best of the visitor season because when we were at Howe Wath we sold a lot of dressed poultry from the door. People who took visitors in and did meals for them needed chickens and ducks, and cream, which we sold as well.

The doctor often used to come for me to help an old couple in Castleton. They were a canny old couple but they were really ailing. If I worked hard all day, for about ten hours, I got a shilling. And I thought that was wonderful because it was a long way towards paying my insurance stamp. When they were really ill and I had to stay the night I got sixpence, because I wasn't working hard! Other people were doing the same sort of thing at the same time, but they didn't all have eight brothers and a Dad to wash for like me. I've known times I've pegged out twenty-eight shirts! That was a couple of days work, because to fetch water to fill the copper we had to collect it from across the road where there was an overflow from somebody else's supply up the hill, and bring it over the road and through the yard to the house. It was the only water we had. A house with no water, not even close, and no electricity. No such thing as a bathroom, and the 'small house' was quite a way off, down at the bottom of the garden! How things have changed since then.

When I came back again here to Westerdale, to help when my brothers rented New House Farm, Uncle John Featherstone and his niece and nephew were still living at Church Farm. My mother said, "You'll have to go and see Lisa Emma", who was Uncle John's niece, and George Willie, her brother, who was a proper character.

I got such a shock when I went to see them ~ it was like another age altogether, they were so quaint, and I was nearly knocked down by dogs that came bolting out of the living room at the back. They had a totally different way of living, dressing, and every day life. The Miss Featherstones were very careful people ~ they must have been to build a house. Being unmarried they'd not had an income from a husband like some people do. Emma took on a part time posting job, and used to walk to Wood End and up to Esklets to take letters to a reporter who wrote every week about country affairs for the Whitby Gazette who lived there, and then they set up a Post Office.

The Miss Featherstones, Frances and Emma, built Rose Cottage, the house where I live now. When we were living at Plum Tree my father brought us back to Westerdale regularly, walking across the moors. I walked on the foundations of Rose Cottage when they were being laid, and I little dreamt then that I would be living in it now in my old age! Rose Cottage was finished in 1923, but they left it for two years to dry out! They moved the Post Office there into the specially built end part.

My brothers farmed at New House until it was sold, very disappointingly, when they had just got it established and made a lovely place of it. That was a shock. In perhaps '42 or '43 Thomas took a farm in Goathland. During their notice to leave (terms then in Westerdale ended on the 25th March) there were terrible snow storms, and I walked up there to New House over the tops of hedges, walls and dykes on the snow for weeks. It started in January, and when it came to term day, the 25th, they couldn't move because there wasn't a road to get a wagon there through the snow to collect even the pigs and so on. It was April before we could move. The sheep we had to leave on the land. The pigs and the hen house went by road. They trucked the cattle from Castleton by train to Egton. Then there was another gang of men at the other end to drive them the other four miles further. It was all such hard work, for very little return. All those winters at New House were such bad ones, with a lot of snow. You couldn't get through Ossiker Crook Wood to follow the road there. You had to come through wherever you could because the snow was high above the hedges where it had blown and drifted, and then frozen hard. It was dry and cold, sunny during the days, but then it would blow it all in at night. Like 1963, that was a bad winter. The children didn't get to school for six weeks, and the Broadgate children used to come to the village and join the rest of them sledging all day long!

I was at home after my brothers moved to Goathland, doing various jobs. Then eventually in 1955 I married Jim, who I'd always known, and came back again to Westerdale to live in Rose Cottage. Jim was from Dale View. His family lived and farmed there for three generations. His grandfather, father, and Jim, Muriel and their brother Tom all lived there.

When I came to Rose Cottage to live, and I'd only been here for three months, the lady who had the village shop down the road where Miss Ruff and Miss Longmuir live now died. After a week or two several people came to my door and asked me to set up a small shop in the little post office part of the house, because there was now nowhere to get bread or the basic things they wanted. So we started up, and I had the little village shop for years and years. By then Westerdale Hall had become a Youth Hostel.

I just sold essentials, mainly, things that fitted in to the small space I had, and with the needs of the Youth Hostellers in mind. I sold a lot of tinned stuff for a handy meal for them, because they'd only got gas rings, and probably kettles provided in the hostel, and if they didn't order a meal they made their own suppers. The hostel didn't open till 5pm, so my busiest time was coming towards 5 o'clock when they were all coming in, and then the next morning when they were all going out after 9. They had to

Westerdale Hall - when a Youth Hostel

leave the hostel by 10am. Then there were the other visitors, the walkers and holiday makers. We had visitors from Holland. I sold a lot of post cards.

When I came here the number coming to the hostel was just under five thousand a year! It was very busy. People couldn't stay there if they came by car at that time, though that changed later. Hostels were only for walkers and cyclists, and for school parties who came by bus. Parties of schools children were booked into the hostel from all over the country, and sometimes I organised with the farmers for the children to go on their land to do field studies and that sort of thing. Half of the children in a school party would be dropped here and the other half would go to the Saltburn hostel to the seaside. Then halfway through the week they would change over. There were fifty beds in the hostel, bunk beds, and there was an enormous boiler to heat the water for all those baths. Showers were installed after I came here, and floors laid, and different wash basins and kitchen sinks. When I first came the kitchen sinks were leaded, and there were enormous wooden draining boards dating from about 1850 when they were put in.

To stock my shop, reps came round, groceries were delivered, and the lemonade man came out from Middlesbrough once a month and the sweet man did too. The hostellers used to like to put a Mars Bar in their bags when they went on their long walks. There were three bread vans a week coming to my shop or the hostel, with loaves, biscuits, cakes and pies. People were constantly asking me for directions and information. I was open every day except Sunday, and even sometimes briefly on Sundays if someone was desperate, though I didn't encourage it!

I had two little children by then, and my mother came here to live in 1960, and she lived here with us for years. My father had become ill, and my sister-in-law, who was a trained nurse, took my parents to Goathland so that she could look after them. He had a very short illness before he died there. He'd always had very good health, and my mother was the same. The only hospital treatment either of them ever had was once a few years before when my father had a broken leg. He was knocked down by a sheep, but he soon got over it. I used to go down to Westerdale Hall to help them with the inventory.

Mary with her daughters

My brother Robert married here in Westerdale. When he was courting Mary he was living in Baysdale, and when the snow was melting over Urrah Moor and the water came rushing down into the hogras, or valleys, it was difficult to get across them to visit her. One part got particularly bogged and heavy with water, so he set to work and built a lovely stone bridge. Roland Close, who lived in the Shepherd's Cottage at Baysdale, helped him. They had to find all the stone. They built the bridge one summer, in their spare time at the end of the days. There's a date stone at both the top of the bridge and at the bottom.

I've had a busy life.

Westerdale C of E School in 1896. *Back, from left*: Maud Bruce, Dora Cockerill, Alice Leng, Alice Cockerill, Sarah (Sally) Atkinson, Hannah Hartley, Lucy Hartley, John Bruce, Fred Frank, David Hartley, George Noble; Laura Frank, James Mortimer, John Thomas Booth, William Bruce, James Lynas, Sanderson Dowey, Alfred Mortimer, Thomas Lynas, William Dale, James Bowes, and teacher Mr William Hardy; Thomas Cook, William Brown, Hannah Dale, Annie Pennock. Mary Jane Hartley, Elizabeth Dale, Ada Pennock, Hannah Mary Dowey, Amy Atcock, Florence Lynas and Ada Lynas; Arthur Noble, Elijah Noble, Walter Booth, John Atkinson, Charlie Cockerill, George Dale, Mary Mercer and Laura Hill.
Laura Hill and Alfred Mortimer became Mary's parents-in-law.

123

How a building has changed - and a very early memory

1

2

3

This is Arkangel, a cottage in Westerdale, as it has altered in over a hundred years. Mrs Francesca Garforth lives there now, and has done so since the mid 1960s.

The first picture is a Frank Meadow Sutcliffe photograph *(thanks to Whitby Museum, WLPS)* and it probably dates from around 1881 when there was only the very old Jane Burrows and her forty old son living there, before the cottages were rebuilt.

The dates of the others are not certain. The cottages were rebuilt as one in 1900 and renamed Arkangel by the then owners Fentriss-Ellerby of Town Farm. Mary Mortimer's parents and their young family were living there for a year or so from about 1907. Emma Beeforth remembers that a Mrs Ackroyd lived there in about 1920 (possibly in the third photo). Mrs Sadie Ellerby (then Adamson) moved here in the 1930s. Mrs Ellerby is in the fourth and the fifth picture.

The last photograph (of Francesca) was taken in 2008.

An older story ...
In most of the photos, including the first, you can see the "Bulmer Stone" which is a monument that was engraved and erected in 1727 by Thomas Bulmer, a mariner, who lived there then.

At that time there was a group of cottages (at least three) and the cluster was known as Town Head. The engraving on the monument is remarkably clear considering it was done by a sailor rather than a mason and nearly 300 years ago. The words and pictures describe much of the life of this unknown mariner - like a very old "conversation". They do not explain how he came to end his days living on the moors - probably this was where he started because it was quite usual for boys and young men of the moorland to walk to the ports to seek employment as sailors. On panels around it there is written:

THO.BVLMER WHO LIVED HERE HAS OFTEN CROSSED THE MAIN.

"27 Sols Tossed on Rovgh Seas on Broken Pieces of The Ship Vntil Daybrake Then They all Escaped Safe to Land. 1727 IN THIS YEAR IT WAS MY TRUE INTENT TO MAKE HERE A LASTING MONNAMENT TO SHOW THY MERCIES EVERYWHERE ABOVND AND SAVES WHERE NO MANKIND ARE TO BE FOUND. OF THIS I HAVE NOW HAD A LARGE EXPIERYANCE. TO MANY FOREIN SHORES THEN GERMANY HOLLAND FRANCE AND SPAIN WRECKED AT LENTH HIS FRAIL BARK. THE HOPEFULL ANCHORS CAST IS NOW UNRIGGED AND HERE LYETH MOORED FAST. REMEMBER MAN THY SAIL ON SEA SHORT IT MUST BE. WE MUST BE STRIPT OF ALL AND THEN RETURN TO DUST. *The Four Ships:*
Y HOPEFUL,
Y FAITHFUL, THIS SHIP THE PROVIDENCE AND THIS THE CHARITY.

THOMAS BULMER - THE ANCIENT MARINER'S MEMORIAL. ARKANGEL COTTAGE

R. H. Hayes 7
WESTERDALE

SOME OF THE STORY TELLERS

DERRICK CHAMPION

I was born on 7th December 1918 at Poppleton near York and at one week old moved back to Rosedale with my parents, brother Alwyn and sister Heather. I went to Rosedale Abbey school. In 1927 we moved to Castleton and I left school at fourteen. I moved into the family garage business and I started up my own haulage business with my donkey. I needed a driving licence to be able to help Father with the garage, and I lost it before I got it! I had to go to court with Father and was charged one pound and eight shillings for under age driving. I passed my test first time later on. We started up a taxi service. It was while running people to the picture house that I met my wife-to-be, Enid, an usherette. We were married for sixty-five years. I sadly lost her in 2005 when she had a short illness and died at eighty seven years old. I joined the services in 1939 as a flight mechanic. After the war I returned to the garage with Father. I went shooting, and bred ponies and a few pigs. The ponies have been a big part of my life and I supported local shows. My ponies Mannequin and Grace won at Wembley and Grace was Pony of the Year there. Since then my ponies have won at the other side of the world, at the Royal Melbourne Show. The garage is still in the family with Rik, Joyce and Ryan and they all enjoy rally driving with great success. I still go shooting, support the hunt, and I recently started a new career appearing in a television advertisement for Muller rice. What comes around the next corner I never know!

FRANK FISHPOOL

I was born in December 1935 at 3 Ashfield Road, Castleton. I was the youngest of three children of Walter and Mary Fishpool. I Attended Castleton Primary School 1940-1946 then Whitby Grammar School till 1951.

During this time I delivered bread for Mrs Codling and papers for Wilsons on a night and Welfords on a Sunday. After I left school I worked for R Scarth at Hareslack farm near Castleton for a year before going to the Quarry for two years. I joined the RAF for 3 years (1954-57) after which I worked for North Yorkshire County Council as a roadman.

I married Mary Scarth in 1962 (she died in 1988) and I left Castleton in 1964 to work at ICI and later for Her Majesty's Customs & Excise, returning to Castleton in 1993, three years after retirement, to live in Ash Lea.

HILDA FLINTOFT

I was born on 2nd of March 1929 at Bilsdale to Fred and Annie Cook. We lived at Blackemires in Danby, and Dad was the sexton at Danby Church. We moved to Ainthorpe and I went to Danby school. When I married Herbert Flintoft we went to live at Mount Pleasant in Castleton and then to Broadgate farm in Westerdale. We have five daughters, seven grand daughters, four grandsons, 2 great grand daughters and 1 great grandson.

ANNIE GAINES

I was born on the 26th of February 1929 at Falcon Farm Danby Dale, the only daughter of Arthur Reginald and Sarah Elizabeth Gaines. I went to school at Danby Church of England school and left at 14 years old. I went to work at Botton Hall for the McMillans as a domestic. I left at the age of 23 to look after mother who was ill. I still worked part time for the McMillans as they owned the farm that father ran. Mother passed away in 1953 at the age of 53. I stayed at the farm until 1955 when my dad and brother Leslie Gaines and myself moved to Castleton as our farm was sold to the Camphill Village Trust. Father passed away in 1978 and my brother died in 1999. I remained doing domestic duties in the Castleton area at Dibble bridge

LINDA GROUT

I was born at "Overdene" in Saltburn and lived at Daleside Farm in Westerdale as a small child. I went to Castleton School driven by Derrick Champion in the school taxi. We moved to Castleton in 1961. My Grandmother, Edith Cobbold and my mother Betty Stonehouse ran the village fish and chip shop. My parents ran the Downe Arms in Castleton from 1965 till 1989. I married Colin, and have three daughters, one grandaughter and one grandson.

ELSIE MOULD

I was born Elsie May Dowey on the 13th of May, 1919 at Hollins Farm in Westerdale. My parents were Albert and Lucy Dowey and my brother was John. I went to Westerdale school, left at 14 years old, and after leaving school worked hard on the farm. There was no other choice but I would have rather have been a hairdresser. I left the farm when I married Alfred Mould at Westerdale church. We lived at Howe Wath in Castleton, where I worked on the farm. We had two children, Marjorie and Michael. My husband died 11 years later, and a year later my mother died so I moved with my children to live with my father in Castleton. I started work at Castleton school and over fourteen years did various jobs, as dinner lady, caretaker, playground supervisor etc. I retired at 65. Both my children are married. Marjorie lives in Knaresborough and Michael in Canada. I have four Grandchildren.

EMMA SKIDMORE

I was born on the 15th of February 1932 at Pinfold then moved to Bagdale, both in Westerdale. My parents were William and Dinah Thompson and I had one sister and three brothers. I went to school at Westerdale and Castleton, and Dad was bell ringer and sexton at Westerdale church. We moved to Dibble Bridge near Westerdale, and I worked at Dibble Bridge and Kildale Hall. I married Allen Skidmore at Westerdale church in 1954. We have one daughter who lived with her husband at Grange Farm in Westerdale. They now live in Castleton, and we have three grandsons.

BETTY TAYLOR

I was born on the 23rd of May 1931 to George and Isabel Earney at Pateley Bridge. I went to school until I was 14 years old, then got a job in Boots the chemist in Harrogate. I came to Castleton for a holiday to my Nan at Maddy Farm on the hill above Dibble Bridge. She was poorly and lonely. I couldn't leave her. I stayed with her at Maddy until she died. I met George Robert Taylor who lived in Westerdale and we married in 1953. I worked for Lady Guisborough at Dibble Bridge, and at Castleton school as cook (not Betty's words but everyone says she was the best ever!) We still live in Castleton. We have two children, Yvonne and Martin, and have three grandchildren and three great grandsons.

BESSIE UNDERWOOD

I was bom in 1925 the eldest child of Wilfred and Elsie Flintoft at Lieth House Farm at Westerdale. I went to Westerdale school until I was twelve and then to Lealholm school for one year. Leaving school at thirteen I worked on the farm until I married Reg Underwood in 1948. We had two sons Robert and Leslie. I worked in houses and at the Downe Arms until my husband and mother needed looking after. When they died I went travelling with my friend Betty Stonehouse to most parts of the world. When we were in Australia I broke my ankle and was taken in the famous flying doctors plane to hospital. I have enjoyed a long and happy life.

(Sadly in 2008 we no longer have Elsie Dowson, Joyce Metcalfe or Bill Beattie with us to enjoy this book - we have fond and grateful memories of them all.)

Some of the Tea Shop Reminiscence Group

*Front left, Elsie Mould, Emma Skidmore, Hilda Flintoft, Georgina Truscott, Frank Fishpool,
Arthur Dowson, and Derrick Champion
Back row from left, Betty Taylor, Annie Gaines, Pam Scarth, Bessie Underwood, Linda
Grout, Gabrielle Lawson*

This project began in the year 2001 in the village of Westerdale where I live, when I began to talk to people whose stories are precious because so few others remember them. I recorded conversations. Linda Grout became involved after the idea to record memories was on a "wish list" that first evolved at public meetings of a North York Moors National Park Farm and Rural Scheme, launched by Prince Charles in 1998 when he visited Danby Parish. In 2005 Chris and Peter Knapp began recording conversations in Danby. Then in 2006, as part of the "Esk Moors Action for the Elderly" Care Plan project, Lottery funding was awarded for the reminiscing meetings, which Linda began on Tuesday mornings in Castleton Tea Shop. I started putting the stories into text. Most of the recordings have been kept safe.

Over ten years ago my husband John and I joined a group of friends and neighbours trying to find ways to help local older people to stay living actively, independently and comfortably here in the Upper Esk Valley instead of moving away to find help when they need it, or doing with less help than they should because of remoteness. It began with the formation of "Esk Moors Action for the Elderly". This voluntary community group evolved to organise what is now known widely as "The Esk Moors Project" to tackle lack of housing, personal care services and transport, and to reduce loneliness. With help from AbbeyfieldUK, it raised funds to build an "Abbeyfield" 'extra care' scheme with twelve flats for local older people and a community centre. It set up "Esk Moors Caring", a registered charity and local social enterprise to provide care to people in their homes and at the Abbeyfield scheme in the Upper Esk Valley, and also to set up and support social activities so that people are not lonely. Any profits from the sale of this book will go to "Esk Moors Caring" so that older people in the Upper Esk Valley will continue to benefit.

My grateful thanks go to Linda Grout, who is also a member of Esk Moors Action for the Elderly, and has been the organiser and hostess for the Tuesday Reminiscence Meetings in Castleton Tea Shop. Linda, like her mother Betty Stonehouse before her, has done so much for her older neighbours. Thanks too to Pam Scarth and other helpers. Thanks to Chris and Peter Knapp, who with friends began Esk Moors Action for the Elderly (and also now run "Esk Moors Active" a sister social enterprise, to run the Heather Hopper mini-bus because there is so little easily accessible public transport in the valley). Thanks go to Age Concern, Scarborough & District for the great support they have given through their worker Gabrielle Lawson, and for funding for most of the coffees and scones. Grateful thanks to Danby Parish Council and the Lottery Microgrants scheme for funding towards making the book. Thanks to Anne Bowes for her advice on publishing. I thank all those who loaned the beautiful photographs for the book. Very grateful thanks to Angela and Steve at Castleton Tea Shop, and to the Kellys at the Moors Centre Tearoom where we sometimes meet. And thank you most of all to the wonderful people you have met in this book.

There are many stories not yet told, and people not yet spoken to. I'm sure the Group will be there at the Tea Shop next Tuesday.

Georgina Truscott
September 2008

Thanks for permission to use postcards to Judges Ltd, Hastings, Whitby Museum and Copyright, Whitby Literary and Philosophical Society, and Ryedale Folk Museum, and for advice from Beck Isle Museum Pickering, Kirkleatham Museum Redcar and Whitby Museum.

Thanks to the Whitby Gazette for permission to use extracts.

I have made every attempt to trace copyright on materials and any infringement is unintentional.

These accounts, photographs and cuttings relate to actual events and memories, and nothing is intended to vitiate or misrepresent any persons, alive or dead.

All proceeds from the sale of this book will go to Esk Moors Caring Ltd, a community led local registered charity (no. 1113392) and social enterprise established in 2006 to make life independent, easier and more active and sociable for older folk living in over sixty square miles of the Upper Esk Valley on the North York Moors.